Animal Parents

Jeremy Cherfas

Lerner Publications Company
Minneapolis

Contents

Introduction

Imagine a male giving birth to the young instead of a female. Or a mother producing young with no father at all. Sound impossible? Not for the male sea horse, which carries eggs in a pouch in his body and takes care of the young. Not for the female desert-grass whiptail lizard, which produces eggs that develop into young lizards without the help of a male.

The sea horse and the whiptail provide only two examples of the incredible number of ways in which animals produce offspring. Once the young are born, animal parents have just as many different ways of raising (or not raising) them. Some parents have only a few offspring and take care of them for a long time. Others produce hundreds or thousands of offspring and immediately leave the young to take care of themselves.

Although they mate and raise their young in ways that may seem strange and different, all animals parents share the same important goal. They try to make sure that their offspring survive and grow to adulthood. What seems like unusual behavior by some parents may actually be the best way to ensure the young's survival.

In this book, we will look at some of the different ways that animal parents bring their young into the world and help them to survive.

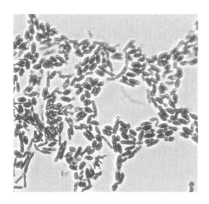

Simple organisms like these tiny bacteria reproduce by splitting in two. In more complex animals, males and females come together to produce young.

Like many birds, these mute swans mate for life. The male and female both provide care for their offspring.

3

1 / Reproduction

Adult animals create offspring by a process know as reproduction. In most animals, this means that a male reproductive cell, called the **sperm**, joins with a female reproductive cell, called an **egg**. The uniting of the sperm and the egg is **fertilization**. Fertilization can occur inside the female parent's body or outside, depending on the **species** of animal.

The **embryo**, or fertilized egg, eventually grows to become the young animal. But that takes time. Animal parents have different ways of feeding and protecting the embryo while it is developing.

Birds, amphibians, and insects, for example, encase the embryo with its own food supply (the **yolk**) in a protective shell or sac, also known as an egg. Even-

Below: This female tabby cat gave birth to her kittens as the final step in the process of reproduction. Like all mammals, she feeds her young with milk produced in her body.

Above: These newborn European red deer twins began life as embryos inside their mother.

tually, the egg may be laid outside the female's body, kept inside the female, or even given to the male to hatch.

Once eggs hatch, the offspring may go through a series of transformations before they become adults. For example, frog eggs hatch as fish-like tadpoles. But they soon develop into adult frogs. Other eggs, such as those of reptiles, may simply produce "baby" versions of the adults they will become over time.

In **mammals** like elephants and humans, the embryo stays inside the female, where it is protected and fed by the female's body. At the end of its period of development, it is ready to be born as a live baby mammal.

A baby elephant grows inside its mother for nearly two years before it is born.

When the sperm fertilizes the egg, certain traits from the parents are combined in the embryo. These traits are called genetic because they are carried in the genes found in the egg and sperm. Genetic traits may include size, strength, coloration, or shape of body features.

In addition to these genetic traits, many young animals learn certain ways of behaving from their parents. Learned behaviors might include such things as the ability to find food or to hide from **predators**. These skills are passed on to offspring to help them survive.

Reproducing for survival

Some animal parents can change their reproductive activity to make sure that the most offspring possible survive and grow to become adults. One way that birds adapt their reproduction is to lay just the right number of eggs.

But what is the right number? In fact, why stop laying eggs at all if the idea is to have as many young survive as possible? The answer is that when it comes to reproduction, more is not necessarily better.

Take the European swift. Like many birds, it is capable of laying a large number of eggs each season. But it doesn't. Normally, most swifts stop laying after three eggs, although some lay only two and others lay four.

Below: An adult European swift feeds insects to four-day-old chicks. The parent birds spend almost all their time collecting food for themselves and their chicks.

Above: Although these young swifts are almost ready to fly, they still need to be fed by their parents.

Like many other birds, the European swift usually lays just the right number of eggs to ensure that the most offspring possible will survive.

Scientific studies have shown that three eggs are the most that a pair of swifts can normally hatch and raise successfully. If the mother laid six eggs, it's likely that three chicks would die before reaching adulthood.

The reason? Feeding hungry chicks takes almost all the parents' time. In a normal year the parents can only catch enough insects to feed three. If they lay four eggs, one or more of the nestlings may starve. When food is plentiful, swifts with four eggs may be able to raise them all successfully. But when food is scarce, even three chicks may be one too many. On average, if swifts lay three eggs, then they will have more young leaving the nest than if they lay either two or four.

Millions of species

There are millions of animal species, and one of the things that makes them different is the way they reproduce. Animals differ in how they have their young, how long the embryos grow, and how the parents care for the embryos and the young. A codfish, for example, produces millions of eggs and provides no care at all, while a female elephant has only six calves during her life and looks after each one carefully.

These methods of reproducing and caring for the young are very different. Yet no one way is better or worse than any other. Each species has arrived at its own special method of reproduction after thousands, even millions, of years of evolution. Whatever the method is, it usually begins with finding a partner.

Many corals look like plants, but they are actually colonies of tiny animals. Some corals produce eggs and sperm that unite to form new coral animals. Others reproduce by a process called budding.

Sea anemones are related to corals and reproduce in similar ways. In some species, fertilization takes place inside the female anemone, and the young anemones develop there. This photograph shows a beadlet anemone releasing young anemones from the opening in its body.

2 / Courtship and Mating

Before many animals reproduce, males and females have to find each other and form pairs. The process of finding and selecting a suitable mate is called courtship. In some animal species, males and females do not have to pair up in order for mating to take place. Some sea anemones, for example, simply release their eggs and sperm into the water at the same time and leave it to luck and the currents to bring them together.

Corals, which are related to sea anemones, often use the same system. All the corals on a particular reef release their reproductive cells at the same time. The process, which is usually triggered by the moon and tides, gives eggs and sperm the best possible chance of meeting.

Most other animals form pairs, but the members of some species don't have to look very hard for a suitable mate. For example, during most of the year, the sea birds known as Abbott's boobies fly all over the Pacific Ocean, searching for fish. When it comes time to mate, however, all the Abbott's boobies in the world head for one tiny speck of land in the South Pacific, Christmas Island. Once they reach the island, the birds have no trouble finding mates.

A pair of boobies with their young

Boobies spend most of their time in the air, roaming far and wide over the Pacific Ocean. When it is time to mate, the birds go to Christmas Island in the South Pacific to find partners.

Sending out signals

To attract a suitable mate, many animals use some kind of signal. Birds sing, frogs croak, and toads call. Animals can also send out signals by smell. Insects, for example, waft powerful perfumes, called pheromones, into the air. But attracting a partner may only be the start. Many animals have a period of courtship, during which they select the most suitable partner.

Courtship—Selecting for Survival

The main goal of animal parents is to ensure their offsprings' survival. During courtship, many animals try to find mates with traits and behaviors that will help their young survive.

A male tree frog in the rain forest of Costa Rica produces a loud mating call by inflating his vocal sac.

A male European song thrush sings a courtship song while perched in a flowering apple tree. Spring is the time of year when many male birds sing to attract mates.

Left: A male common tern offering a fish to a female he is courting. This is known as courtship feeding.

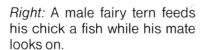

Right: A male fairy tern feeds his chick a fish while his mate looks on.

For example, the female common tern looks for a mate that is a good fisherman. This is because the male must catch fish and bring them to her when she is **incubating** her eggs. Later, when the eggs have hatched, both parents will have to find food to satisfy the young birds. During courtship, the male often brings the female a present of a few fish to prove his skill. If two males are courting one female, she usually chooses the male that brings her the most fish.

In other bird species, such as the great argus pheasant, the males mate with many different females and do not help to take care of the chicks. For these birds, appearance is very important in courtship. The more attractive a male, the better his chances of mating with many females. If his sons inherit their father's attractiveness, then they will also mate in their turn with many females.

When he is courting, a male argus pheasant tries to appear at his most attractive. He shows off his gorgeous spotted feathers, leaping up and down in the middle of a clearing and calling. A female may visit several males and watch each performance before she chooses a mate.

Even though the male pheasant does not help the female to raise their young, choosing the most attractive male gives the female's offspring the best chance of success.

A male great argus pheasant from Malaysia. He is displaying his gorgeous fan of feathers to impress the plain-looking female in the foreground.

Several male ruffs display to a single female bird. The males also stage mock fights to impress a female. Ruffs are European birds related to sandpipers.

A male and female toad mating. At the same time that the large female (bottom) lays her eggs, the smaller male releases sperm to fertilize them. Toads are amphibians. They live most of the year on dry land but reproduce in water.

Making choices

In most species, it is the female that selects a mate. Males are generally anxious to mate. Females, on the other hand, may need time and much persuasion to decide on a partner. This is because females usually invest so much in reproduction.

A female toad, for example, needs extra food so that her body can produce eggs and supply them with nutritious yolks. She can't afford to choose a weak male that might produce weak offspring. Otherwise, all the energy she used in preparing for reproduction would be wasted. The female would have to survive another year before she could breed again. So she is careful to find a strong, healthy mate.

A male toad, like many male animals, does not have to spend as much energy to get ready for reproduction. Instead of looking for just the right mate, he tries to mate with many females.

A bull elephant seal (shown here with females and pups) mates with as many females as he can and fights off other bulls.

A red deer stag bellows to warn other stags not to come near the females in his herd.

Mating systems

In some species, each female mates with as many males as she can, and each male mates with as many females as he can. In general, however, females put their effort into producing eggs and raising young, while males compete for females.

The most common system of mating is called **polygyny**, which roughly means "many females." In polygynous species, each male tries to mate with several females, although some may end up mating with none. To help them win the competition for females, polygynous males are often large, with weapons like fangs, horns, or antlers. Elephant seals and red deer are examples of polygynous animals.

Another mating system is called **polyandry,** which means "many males." It is very rare in the animal world. When it does happen, the females tend to behave like the males of polygynous species. There are a few polyandrous birds but no polyandrous mammals.

The final type of mating system is called **monogamy,** which means "one mate." A monogamous animal has only one partner and often stays with it for life. In monogamous species, the male and female often look quite similar and behave in similar ways. The fox, the beaver, the gibbon, and many birds are monogamous.

Foxes are monogamous mammals. A fox usually has the same mate for life.

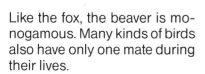

Like the fox, the beaver is monogamous. Many kinds of birds also have only one mate during their lives.

3 / *Patterns of Parenthood*

Just as animal parents have different ways of reproducing, they also have different ways of raising the young. For example, the male red kangaroo spends most of his energy fighting to keep other males away from a female that is ready to mate. Once he mates, the male has little to do with raising the young kangaroos.

The male stickleback, a small fish about six inches long, does help to raise his offspring. A male defends a **territory** against other males, and he also builds a nest for the young. Made from plant material, the nest is held together with a sticky substance produced by the male stickleback's body. The female lays her eggs in this nest and then leaves. The male fertilizes the eggs and stays near the nest, guarding the eggs and fanning water over them. He also protects the eggs from predators.

Kangaroos are marsupials, animals that carry their young in pouches after they are born. Male kangaroos do little to help the females raise the young kangaroos, which are known as joeys.

The male three-spined stickleback fans water over his eggs and protects them from predators.

This egg laid by a small shark known as a dogfish is surrounded by a tough case or capsule. Like many shark eggs, it is equipped with threads that catch on underwater plants and keep it from drifting.

How do parents provide care?

Guarding is just one of the many ways in which animals provide parental care. They also provide food. All birds lay eggs that contain a good food supply, the yolk, to nourish the growing embryo. Pigeons provide another kind of food. The male and female both produce a nourishing liquid from special cells in their throats. After they hatch, the young pigeons drink this "milk."

Some parents have many young and give them only a little care. Other have fewer offspring but look after each one carefully. When a codfish **spawns**, it may lay from four to six million eggs. Each egg gets only a little yolk and no protection from predators. Only one or two young codfish usually survive to adulthood.

Sharks have fewer young but give each one a lot of care. Some sharks keep their eggs inside their bodies and give birth to live young, but most lay eggs, perhaps 20 or 25 each year. The eggs are large, with plenty of yolk to feed the embryos. They have a tough covering to protect them. Even though the female shark produces few eggs, each of them has a good chance of surviving.

Pigeon parents provide a nourishing milky liquid for their young to drink after they hatch. The pigeon shown here is a pet being held by its owner.

17

Who looks after the young?

There seem to be three basic patterns of parenthood in the animal world. In many species of animals, both parents leave their offspring to survive on their own. In other species, one parent leaves and the other looks after the young.

With fish, it is often the male that is left holding the baby. For example, the female stickleback leaves the male to look after their young. But in guppies, the brightly colored fish so common in tropical aquariums, the female keeps the eggs inside her and gives birth to live young.

In the third system of parental care, both parents share the job of looking after their offspring. Most birds use this system, but it occurs in only a few fishes and mammals. For example, gibbons, the small apes that live in Southeast Asia, live in family groups that consist of a mother and father and their offspring. Both male and female provide care for the young.

Like many fish, the bluehead wrasse lays its eggs and leaves them to survive on their own.

Male and female gibbons share the work of raising their young.

4 / Offspring on Their Own

Animal parents that leave their offspring on their own do many things to improve their chance of survival. The bullfrog offers a good example of how absent parents provide for their young.

Bullfrogs first select a safe place to lay their eggs. In fact, choosing good egg-laying places is part of courtship and mating for this species. The males fight for good breeding places, and the females choose mates that have won that fight.

But even the best breeding pond will have some predators. So after mating, female bullfrogs try to find a place to lay their eggs where predators will not eat them.

The main predator of bullfrog eggs is the leech.

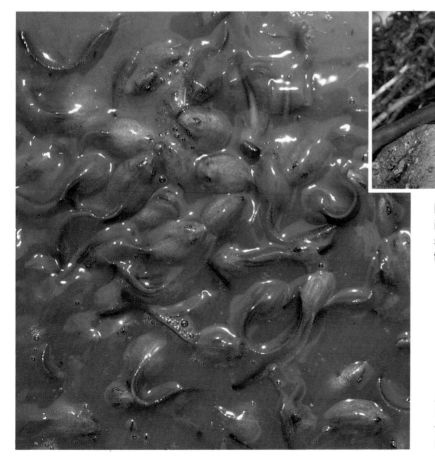

Bullfrog parents lay their eggs in places where they will be safe from predators such as this leech (above).

After they hatch from their eggs, bullfrog tadpoles (left) complete their development without the help of their parents.

To save the eggs from leeches, the female selects a place where the water is shallow and rather warm. Eggs grow more quickly in warm water. This gives the leeches less time to eat the eggs before they hatch into tadpoles and swim away.

The female also protects her eggs against leeches by finding a spot with few water plants. If there are many plants, the eggs cannot form a clump. Where there are fewer plants, the eggs gather into a ball. The leeches have a harder time eating the balled-up eggs than they do single eggs.

Even though bullfrogs do not look after their eggs and young, they do lay the eggs where they have the best chance of growing into adults. Other animals do the same thing. Green turtles that live along the coast of Brazil swim thousands of miles to lay their eggs on the safe beaches of Ascension Island. The female digger wasp abandons her eggs but leaves a supply of paralyzed caterpillars to provide food for the young wasps after they hatch.

Below: The female green turtle swims thousands of miles to lay her eggs on the sandy beaches of Ascension Island, in the middle of the South Atlantic Ocean.

Above: After laying 100 to 200 eggs, the green turtle buries them in the sand. When the young turtles hatch, they dig themselves out and head for the sea.

5 / Care by One Parent

For many species, letting offspring raise themselves is not a good survival method. Abandoning eggs or live young, even in a nest or burrow, can be dangerous because predators might find and eat them. For these animals, at least one parent is needed to care for the offspring.

As we have seen, one common way that a parent provides care is by guarding the eggs or the young. But even that may not be enough. To better protect offspring, many animals shelter their eggs and young inside their own bodies. Among mammals, it is the female that keeps the young inside her body. In a few other species, the male shelters the young.

The echidna is an unusual mammal that lays eggs. The eggs hatch inside the female echidna's pouch, and the babies continue their development there. This photograph shows a young echidna inside its mother's pouch.

A marsupial like the kangaroo, the female koala carries her baby in her pouch for six months. For the next six months, it rides around on her back.

Animal fathers

We have already met the female guppy, a fish that keeps her eggs inside her body until they hatch. In sea horses, another species of fish, the male carries the eggs and looks after the young. A male sea horse has a special bag in his body called a brood pouch. After mating, the female sea horse injects the fertilized eggs into the brood pouch through a small slit.

Within the brood pouch, the eggs hatch quickly. The baby sea horses do not leave the pouch immediately but stay safely inside, eating bits of skin from a special area. When the young sea horses are big enough, the father "gives birth" by squirting them out through the brood pouch slit. Thanks to the parental care of their father, the young sea horses have a good start in life.

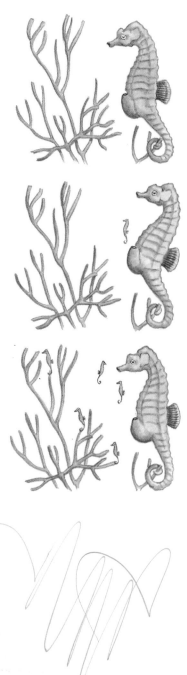

A male sea horse with an enlarged brood pouch containing young sea horses (left). After the young complete their development, they will be released through the slit in the pouch (above).

A male African jacana inspecting a clutch of eggs. In all species of jacanas, the males incubate the eggs and care for the young after they hatch.

Another species in which the male cares for the offspring is the purple jacana. This bird breeds in Central America. It has enormously long toes, which help it run over the leaves of water lilies and other plants that grow in the ponds where it nests. (This is why the purple jacana is sometimes called a lily trotter.)

The female jacana defends a large territory, fighting with other females to keep them away. Four or five males build nests within one female's territory. The female mates with each male and then lays eggs in his nest. After laying the eggs, she has nothing more to do with them. The males incubate the eggs. When the chicks hatch, the fathers protect them until they can look after themselves.

The jacana is one of the few species in which one female mates with several males. In jacanas and sea horses and in most species where the males provide parental care, the females behave almost like males of other species. They are bigger, more brightly colored, and more aggressive. That is because the females have to compete with one another to get males to look after their offspring.

Animal mothers

In most species, it is the female that look after the young. This is especially true among mammals. A female mammal not only protects the young within her body before birth but also provides them with milk once they are born.

Milk is a very good food. For example, a female grey seal feeds her pup milk for only 17 or 18 days, but in that time the pup's weight increases three times, to nearly 110 pounds (50 kilograms). Then the pup, looking like a barrel of blubber, is left alone while the mother goes off to feed. Only when the young seal becomes hungry does it enter the water and start looking for fish. The fat stored from its mother's milk lasts until it can feed itself.

Some mothers feed sons and daughters differently. A red deer stag grows larger if he gets more food as a fawn. A big stag is more likely to mate with many females and produce many offspring. So the urge for survival leads female deer to give their sons more milk than their daughters.

Right: A red deer mother provides milk to feed her young.

Left: A grey seal pup receiving milk from its mother. Seal milk, like the milk of all sea mammals, is very rich and nourishing.

6 / *Care by Two Parents*

In the majority of mammal species, the mother provides most of the parental care. Among birds, both parents take on the job. This is probably because young birds need extra amounts of care to survive. For one thing, the eggs must be incubated and kept safe from predators. Once the eggs hatch, the chicks still need warmth and protection, as well as large amounts of food.

Blue tits, for example, usually have a clutch of 10 nestlings and bring each one some food every 5 minutes or so. This means that the parents have to catch something for their hungry brood about every 30 seconds.

Sometimes, both parents share all the jobs. Herring gulls take turns incubating the eggs. While one sits on the nest, the other searches for food. Later, when the chicks have hatched, the parents continue to take turns. One defends the chicks, while the other brings them food. Perhaps because they do the same jobs, male and female herring gulls look so much alike that it is very difficult to tell them apart.

Blue tit parents have to work hard. They bring food for one of their chicks every 30 seconds.

Herring gull parents take turns incubating the eggs.

Hornbills, birds that live in Africa and India, have a different system of job sharing. The female builds a nest in a hollow tree. As soon as she settles down to lay her eggs, the male seals her into the nest with mud. He builds a thick wall with a small hole through which her long bill can poke.

With the female sealed in and safe from predators, the male goes off to gather food. He brings lizards, insects, and other things to eat and offers them to her through the hole.

Once the chicks hatch, the father smashes down the wall and lets the female out. Then it is the chicks' turn to be sealed up. Both parents bring food to their hungry brood. When the chicks are ready to fly, the parents break down the wall for the last time, and the entire family flies off together.

A male red-billed hornbill feeding his mate. The female is incubating her eggs while sealed inside a hollow tree.

Kittiwakes build nests on steep cliffs along the seacoast. Both parents incubate the eggs and take care of the young. Older pairs of birds are able to raise more chicks because of their long experience as parents.

Practice makes perfect

Bringing up babies is a hard job, especially when the parents must work together. Some animals—for example, kittiwakes—improve with practice.

Kittiwakes, birds related to gulls, are monogamous, mating for life. As a pair gets older, the birds gain more and more experience in caring for their young. This skill allows them to raise more chicks than young parents.

If a kittiwake pair ever fails to breed, the two birds will probably split up and look for new mates. But when they find new partners, they lose the parenting experience gained with their previous mates. The new pairs are no more successful as parents than much younger birds that are breeding for the first time.

27

Monogamous mammals

Monogamy is the exception, not the rule, among mammals. Even when a pair stays together for life, the male may do little to raise the offspring. This is true of the blue duiker, a tiny antelope that lives in the forests of Africa. A pair of blue duikers mates for life and defends its territory against other pairs. But the male does not stay near the female or help her when she has a calf. Instead, he simply guards the territory and acts as a lookout. While he provides some protection for the mother and calf, the father does little else for his family.

Leadbeater's possum, a rare species of marsupial from Australia, has a similar family life. The female builds a large nest in a hollow tree in the middle of a territory and keeps other female Leadbeater's possums out. She allows one male to share her territory, which has a good supply of food—tree gum and sap, as well as insects. But the male does little to help the female care for their young.

Leadbeater's possums live in the tall forests of Victoria, in Australia. In 1921, these little marsupials were thought to be **extinct**, but in 1961, the species was rediscovered.

A female Leadbeater's possum shares her territory with a single male. This rare Australian animals is related to the opposum that lives in North America.

A female duiker and her baby. Duikers mate for life, but the male does not help the female care for the young.

A very caring father

Among the three species of titi monkeys in South America, the males play a very important role in caring for the young. A male and female have a territory in the forest that they defend against others of their kind. Once the female has given birth, usually to one or two infants, the father provides most of the care.

The male carries his offspring through the trees, occasionally handing them over to the mother to nurse. If it is stormy, he hunches over the infants to protect them from the rain. The father also protects his offspring from danger. A scientist once saw a young titi monkey fall out of a tree. Quickly, its father rushed down and sat on the ground near the stunned youngster, guarding it until it was able to climb back into the trees.

The members of a titi monkey family often sit next to one another with their tails entwined. They look like a very contented family. The result of all this care is that titi monkeys probably raise more offspring successfully than other similar species.

Male titi monkeys provide most of the care for the young. Titi monkeys live high in the trees of South American forests and are rarely seen. The species is endangered.

Mother's little helpers

Sometimes parents have extra help in bringing up young. Among silverbacked jackals in Africa, one pup often stays with its parents for a year to help raise its younger brothers and sisters. The "helper" guards the young when the adults are away hunting. It brings food for the mother when she is busy nursing the pups. Later, when the pups are ready to eat solid food, the helper brings them food as well. This assistance pays off. Without a helper, a pair of silverbacks is lucky to raise one pup each year. With a helper, the parents can raise up to three pups.

Older animals may provide also help. In animals with long lives, like elephants and chimpanzees, grandmothers look after their grandchildren. The older animals remember where the family can find food and water in times of hardship. Among chimpanzees, an older female will rush to her daughter's aid when she is threatened by another chimp.

Whether the parents are absent or whether one or both give care, all animal parents try to help their offspring survive. If they are successful, the young will grow to become the next generation of animal parents.

An adult silverbacked jackal with a pup. Young silverbacked jackals help their parents to raise their younger brothers and sisters.

Glossary

egg: a female reproductive cell. The word is also used to refer to the protective shell or sac that encloses the embryo of a bird, reptile, or amphibian.

embryo: a fertilized egg, which will develop into a new animal

extinct: no longer in existence

fertilization: the union of a male sperm and a female egg

incubate: to keep an egg warm so that it will hatch

mammal: a warm-blooded animal usually covered with fur or hair. Female mammals produce milk to feed their young.

monogamy: a mating system in which an animal has a single mate, often for life

polyandry: a mating system in which one female mates with several males

polygyny: a mating system in which one male mates with several females

predator: an animal that kills and eats other animals

spawn: to produce and deposit eggs, especially in large numbers

species: a group of animals with many characteristics in common. Members of one species usually cannot breed with members of other species.

sperm: a male reproductive cell

territory: an area of land in which an animal or group of animals lives. Animals mark out and defend their territories.

yolk: the material in an egg that supplies food for a developing embryo

Index

Pages shown in *italic* type include pictures of the animals.

Library of Congress Cataloging-in-Publication Data

Cherfas, Jeremy.
   Animal parents / Jeremy Cherfas.
      p. cm. — (How animals behave)
   Includes index.
   Summary: Describes the many ways that animal
parents care for their young and try to ensure their
survival to adulthood.
   ISBN 0-8225-2251-9
   1. Parental behavior in animals—Juvenile literature.
[1. Animals—habits and behavior.] I. Title. II. Series:
Cherfas, Jeremy. How animals behave.
QL762.C44   1991
591.51—dc20   90-44260
                                        CIP
                                        AC

Acknowledgments
The publishers wish to thank the following photographers and agencies whose photographs appear in this
book. The photographs are credited by page number and
position on the page (T-top, B-bottom, L-left, R-right).

Ardea London Ltd.: Kenneth Fink, 12T; J. H. Labat,
16T; John Daniels, 17B. Bruce Coleman Ltd.: Alfred
Pasieka, 3T; Jane Burton, 3B, 4B, 16B, 18T; A. J. Deane,
6B; Kim Taylor, 10B; M. P. L. Fogden, 10T; Gunter
Ziesler, 12B, 26; James Simon, 15B; Jen and Des Bartlett,
14T, 19B, 21T, 22, 28B; Rod Williams, 28T; L. C. Marigo,
29; David Hosking, 7, 11T, 27. Frank Lane Picture
Agency: R. P. Lawrence, 4T; G. Moon, 11B; R. Bender,
14B; T. Grewcock, 15T; Frank Lane, 18B, 24T; Michael
Rose, 19T; Silvestris, 20T; Derek A. Robinson, 24B; Fritz
Polking, 30. Nature Photographers Ltd.: Hugo van
Lawick, 5; David Callan, 6T; Don Smith, 8T; Owen
Newman, 13; S. C. Bisserot, 17T; P. Roberts, 20B; Ron
Croucher, 25T; Philip Newman, 25B. NHPA: C. and S.
Pollitt, 21B; Nigel Dennis, 23. Planet Earth: Chris
Howes, 8B; Richard Beales, 9T, 9B.
Front cover photograph: © Gerry Ellis/Ellis Wildlife
Collection

Editorial planning by Jollands Editions
Designed by Alison Anholt-White
Color origination by Golden Cup Printing Co., Ltd.,
Hong Kong
Printed in Great Britain by Eagle Colourbooks Ltd.

Bound in the United States of America

WELCOME
— to our —
TABLE

For Barney, Noah, Toby, Sol, Columba, and Remy
L·M· and E·S·

To my wonderful husband, James
H·L·

First published 2023 by Nosy Crow Ltd.

Nosy Crow Ltd
Wheat Wharf, 27a Shad Thames,
London, SE1 2XZ, UK

This edition published 2023 by Nosy Crow Inc.
145 Lincoln Road,
Lincoln, MA 01773, USA

www.nosycrow.com

Library of Congress Catalog Card Number 2023930530
ISBN 979-8-88777-018-5

Nosy Crow and associated logos are trademarks
and/or registered trademarks of Nosy Crow Ltd.
Used under license.

Text © Laura Mucha and Ed Smith 2023
Illustrations © Harriet Lynas 2023

Series based on an original idea by Moira Butterfield.

Printed in Malaysia
Papers used by Nosy Crow are made from wood
grown in sustainable forests.

1 3 5 7 9 8 6 4 2

WELCOME
— to our —
TABLE

WRITTEN BY
LAURA MUCHA and ED SMITH

Laura has traveled to every continent of the world and writes books of poems, facts, and stories for children. Ed writes lip-smacking recipes in his cookbooks for adults. They're both fascinated by the many different things we humans grow, cook, and eat. They also share and enjoy many meals around the same table (they're married), so decided to join forces to create this book.

ILLUSTRATED BY
HARRIET LYNAS

Harriet was born and raised in Korea. She loved doodling and decided to become an illustrator at the age of ten. She made that dream come true and now illustrates children's books. When she is not drawing, she enjoys cooking exotic foods and walking in the countryside. She lives with her husband and their son in Cambridge, England.

TOMATOES

DOLMA

SOY SAUCE

CARROTS

PASTA

ARTICHOKE

WALNUT

CONTENTS

ROTI

APPLES

HALVA

PEAS

ORANGES

YAMS

BUTTER

PLANTAIN

OKRA

CHOCOLATE

MANGOES

EGGS

*This book is packed
with lots of different
ingredients and dishes
from around the world.
You can find a list of all
the countries included
on page 64.*

FLOUR

MOONCAKES

YOGURT

EGGPLANT

MUSSELS

KIMCHI

INTRODUCTION

We all eat food. Every one of us.

Lots of us think about food too. Is it lunchtime yet?
What will we have for dinner?
Will there be dessert?

But do you ever *really* think about food? Like, how and where does rice grow?
Why does some cheese smell so bad? What exactly is a nut?!

There are almost eight billion humans and 195 countries on the planet.
This book includes just some of the many different types of food that
people grow, cook, and eat in some of those places—otherwise
it would be thousands of pages long!

WE ARE DIFFERENT.

BUT WE ALL LOVE FOOD.

Food doesn't just give us energy. It brings us together, and forms cultures and traditions. By learning about food, you can learn not only about different countries, but also how people have moved around and taken their favorite foods with them.

This book shows how children around the world eat the same things, the same things cooked differently, and different things altogether. It will introduce you to ingredients and dishes that you haven't heard of, let alone eaten before. But perhaps you'll want to. And hopefully you will!

Food is an AMAZING way to travel and explore the globe. So grab your knife and fork, chopsticks, or fingers, and let's dig in.

WELCOME TO OUR TABLE!

We have included lots of words from around the world. If any look tricky to say, you can use the pronunciation guides provided.

SETTING THE TABLE

What do you use to eat your food?

Silverware? Fingers? An edible plate?! Here are some of the ways children around the world move food to their mouths.

KNIFE

FORK

In Europe, North and South America, and Australasia, children usually use a knife and fork when they eat meals. They use the knife to cut food before lifting it to their mouths with the fork.

SPOON

Spoons are also very useful for eating wobbly food like jello!

Sometimes children don't use a knife. Instead they use a fork and spoon — for example, when eating FESENJOON *(fess-en-joon)*, a chicken stew from Iran.

And sometimes they just use a spoon — because it's the best thing to hold liquids like soups and broths, or loose foods like PORRIDGE and CONGEE *(con-jee)*.

CHOPSTICKS

FLAT-BOTTOMED SPOON

Spoons come in all materials, shapes, and sizes. Some are small and dainty with curved bottoms. Others, like those used in Japan and China, have flat bottoms and high sides. This is helpful for holding as much scrumptious SOUP as possible!

Chopsticks come in twos. Each pair of sticks are the same length, but thinner at one end. They're the traditional way to eat food in East Asian countries including China, Japan, South Korea, and Vietnam — and for eating their cuisine around the world. You eat by pinching the chopsticks together to pick up food or shovel it into your mouth.

HANDS

More than a quarter of the world eat mostly with their hands. For children in countries like India, Bangladesh, Pakistan, and Bhutan, their fingers are the main utensil for mixing food and putting it in their mouth.

And for children in Nigeria and South Korea, fingers are the most popular way to eat pounded YAM and EGUSI *(eh-goo-see)* SOUP and SSAMBAP *(sam-bap)* LETTUCE WRAPS.

Even in countries where people mostly use knives, forks, and spoons, fingers can be the most useful tools when eating certain things — like PIZZA in Italy.

In Laos, we use our hands to squish sticky rice into a ball, before dipping it into sauce. Yum!

In many countries, instead of fingers or silverware, children use bread to scoop vegetables and swipe up stews.

In Mexico, TORTILLAS *(tor-tee-yas)* accompany most meals to mop up juices. In Indonesia, flaky, stretchy ROTI *(roh-tee)* are the perfect way to eat soupy DAL. And in Ethiopia, INJERA *(in-jeh-ra)* is both a plate and scoop for the different vegetables, lentils, and stews that sit on top of it.

Injera is like an edible plate! We tear off pieces to scoop up stews.

ROTI

Happy eating!

In many countries, the cook or the host often says something before everyone begins their meal.

Do you say anything before you eat, or do you dive right in?

BON APPÉTIT!
(boh-na-peh-tee)
"Enjoy your meal"
in French

KEU A KA 'ONO!
(kayoo ah kah oh-noh)
"Bon appétit"
in Hawaiian

SMAČNÓHO!
(smatch-no-ho)
"Let it be tasty for you"
in Ukrainian

TË BËFTË MIRË!
(ter berft meer)
"May the food do you good"
in Albanian

SAHTAIN!
(sa-tain)
"Double your health"
in Lebanese

KIA MĀKONA!
(kee-a maah-ko-na)
"Eat well"
in Māori
(spoken in New Zealand)

HA KUU MACAANAATO!
(ha koo ma-aan-tou)
"Have a nice meal"
in Somali

9

WHAT'S YOUR FLAVOR?

How do we taste food?

Although we eat food using our mouths, we actually experience it in many ways. Flavor is a combination of taste, smell, and physical sensations like temperature and tingling. And there are some foods that can trick us into thinking they're burning hot, when actually they're not!

Our tongues sense five different tastes:

SWEET
Sweet means sugary things like strawberries, syrups, and cakes. Long ago, when people had to search for their food in the wild, a sweet taste would have told their tongue that they'd found an ingredient packed with energy. Nowadays, sweet food is much easier to get hold of so we have to be careful — too much sugar can lead to health problems.

SALTY
Salty food like pretzels, bacon, and chips can be tasty . . . as long as they're not TOO salty. That's because too much salt can be dangerous. In other words, by helping us taste, our tongue can also keep us safe!

SOUR
Sour means things that are acidic like lemons and vinegar. Sometimes sour can be great. But, if your tongue thinks something is too sour, it may be that an ingredient you're eating has gone bad and could be harmful for you.

UMAMI (oo-mah-mee)
You can taste umami in foods like tomatoes, mushrooms, and soy sauce — and often it leaves us wanting more. That's because it's in savory foods that are usually good for us.

BITTER
A small amount of bitterness can be nice — a twist of orange peel, a forkful of kale. But, if something is VERY bitter, it can mean that it's poisonous. That's why our tongues notice and dislike the taste.

HOT

COLD

Tingling hot or freezing cold?

As well as sensing taste, your tongue has receptors that tell your brain if food is burning hot or freezing cold. But some ingredients — like chili peppers, mustard, and horseradish — trigger the same receptors. So your brain may think your mouth is burning, even though it's not. And others, like mint, include something called "menthol," which convinces your tongue that it's cold!

There are also a lot of spices that will make your lips and tongue buzz, fizz, and feel numb. One example is Sichuan peppercorns. In China, where they come from, the sensation is known as *ma la*, which means "tingling hot."

SUPERBLY SMELLY

Did you know you eat food with your nose?!

Whenever you think something you're eating is fruity, floral, or spicy, you're describing its flavor. And flavor mostly comes through our nose! Our sense of smell is SO powerful that it can make us hungry. That's why some stores pump out smells — they're trying to make us buy their food!

Some foods are seriously stinky, but we still enjoy eating them. Would you like to try any of these?

DURIAN
(juor-ree-uhn)
This fruit is absolutely packed with goodness. But it's illegal for people in Singapore to carry it on public transportation!

NATTO
(na-toe)
Natto is a Japanese dish made from soybeans that is sticky, slimy, and smelly. Lots of people eat it because it's good for you, but they don't always enjoy the experience!

VIEUX BOULOGNE
(vyuh boo-loyn)
Many cheeses have a strong smell, but some people think this cheese from France is the smelliest of all. Its odor has been compared to a farmyard, rotting leaves, and manure.

STINKING TOE FRUIT
The West Indian locust tree is also known as the "stinking toe tree." Not only do its seed pods look like big toes, but they also smell like them once you crack open the shell.

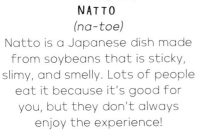

SURSTRÖMMING
(suh-stru-ming)
The fish in Sweden's surströmming has been fermented, which is why it smells so strong (surströmming literally means "sour herring"). But don't worry, not all canned fish is this smelly!

LET'S TALK ABOUT TEXTURE
Foods that are slurpy, spiky, or sticky . . .

Texture is as important as flavor. Food feels very different depending on whether you have to chew, chomp, or slurp it. Which of these textures do you know and enjoy?

CHICKEN FEET
There isn't much meat on chicken feet! In fact, they're really just skin, bone, and something bumpy called "cartilage." They're popular in China, where an important part of enjoying food is its *kougan* or "mouth feel." Eating chicken feet means gnawing, chewing, and savoring the texture, as well as any flavors they've been cooked in.

JELLO
From Belgium to Brazil, Cambodia to Canada, foods with a jelly-like texture are popular across the world. Sometimes they're bouncy, gooey, and gummy, and need to really be chewed. Sometimes they're slippery, and you can slurp them through your teeth.

CHIPS
Chips are thin, crunchy, and . . . CRISP! Some of them can also be greasy because of the oil they're fried in. They're particularly popular in France, the UK, and the US.

Crunchy is . . .

KNACKIG
(k-nack-ig)
in German

CRUIXENT
(croo-shent)
in Catalan

MKARMECH
(me-karr-mesh)
in Arabic, spoken
in Algeria

KNAPRIG
(k-nar-prig)
in Swedish

Chewy is . . .

GOMMOSO
(go-moh-zo)
in Italian

ŽVÝKACÍ
(zh-wee-kats-ee)
in Czech

TAAI
(tie)
in Afrikaans,
spoken in
South Africa

Sticky is . . .

MELEKIT
(muh-luh-keed)
in Malay

GLUDIOG
(glee-dee-og)
in Welsh

Lumpy is . . .

GÆTITTA
(guy-t-eeta)
in Sinhalese, spoken
in Sri Lanka

KEKKJÓTTUR
(khek-yott-urh)
in Icelandic

GLUANT
(gloo-on)
in French

CI LAP LAP
(chee lap lap)
In Cantonese, spoken
in Hong Kong

HALVA
(hal-va)
Halva is eaten in Middle Eastern countries like Cyprus, Lebanon, and Turkey. You can add other ingredients for flavor, but it's made mostly from seed or nut paste and sugar. It's crumbly, chalky, and grainy.

CRÈME BRÛLÉE
(crem broo-lay)
If you want to get to the silky custard in a traditional French *crème brûlée*, you need to shatter the crisp and crunchy top first. SMASH!

PASTA
Spaghetti and other Italian pasta shapes are slippery and smooth. This can make it difficult to eat them without slurping!

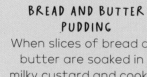

BREAD AND BUTTER PUDDING
When slices of bread and butter are soaked in a milky custard and cooked, they create a traditional English dessert called "pudding" that's spongy, soft, and smooth.

BILTONG
(bill-tong)
Most of the time, food isn't very nice to eat if it has dried out. But there are some meaty snacks that are deliberately dry, leathery, and tough. It can take a lot of effort to eat biltong from South Africa, but it's worth it!

BOBA
A popular drink in Taiwan is bubble tea — but the "bubbles" aren't full of air. They're bouncy, springy, and chewy little balls called *"boba,"* and children suck them up through wide straws. Boba are made from tapioca, which comes from a root vegetable called cassava (see page 25).

REMARKABLE RICE

Have you eaten your rice yet?

In many Southeast Asian countries, asking whether someone has eaten their rice yet is another way of asking "how are you?".

Humans eat on average 155 pounds of rice per person, per year. That's the weight of an adult! In some parts of the world, people eat up to three times that amount.

Of all the plants that are grown for humans to eat, rice is one of the most important. And there are more than 40,000 varieties, from fluffy to sticky, long to short, black to red!

Grains of rice are actually the seeds of a type of grass. Farmers plant the grass in fields that are flooded with water. The grass loves the soggy environment, and the water also keeps pests away.

As the grass grows, the ground dries — either naturally or because farmers drain the field. Eventually, the ground is dry enough to walk on and the rice grains are plump enough to be harvested. Farmers then cut and collect the grass, often by hand. That means growing rice takes a LOT of work.

Next, the grass is beaten to knock the seeds out. But it's still not rice as we know it just yet . . .

The seeds then have to be dried out and separated from their outer coats.

That's a lot of effort for one grain of rice . . . especially when a bowl might contain as many as 5,000!

From field to fork.

BIRYANI *(bih-ree-yah-nee)* is an Indian dish where fragrant rice is layered with potatoes, spices, and meat, then topped with pastry dough. This pastry "lid" keeps the steam and flavors in the pot until everything is cooked and the lid is removed.

JOLLOF RICE *(joll-off)* is a mix of rice, spice, chilies, onions, and tomatoes. It will almost always be on the table at parties and gatherings in Nigeria and Ghana.

RISOTTO *(ri-so-toe)* is a creamy rice dish from Italy. To get the right texture, you must, must, MUST keep stirring as you cook, because this helps it become really oozy.

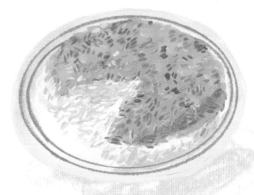

In Iran, rice is sometimes served with **TAHDIG** *(taa-deeg)*. This is when a crisp golden layer from the bottom of the pan is served on top of the fluffy grains. Everyone will want a piece!

CONGEE *(con-jee)* is rice that's boiled for a long time until it's very soft and watery. In China, people often eat congee for breakfast with eggs, fish, or pickled vegetables.

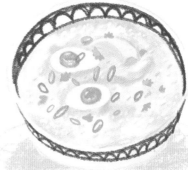

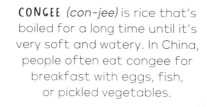

In Spanish, **PAELLA** *(pa-eh-yah)* is the name of a round shallow pan with a flat bottom — and that's exactly what paella is cooked and served in. It's made from rice, peppers, saffron, and either meat, shellfish, or both! If it's cooked well, there will be a crusty layer of rice at the bottom.

Little grains of rice are BIG in Thailand. Rice is eaten with a lot of meals, but it can also be the main part of a dish. **KHAO NIAOW MA MUANG** *(cow nee-ow muh mu-ang)* is a dessert made from sticky rice that is cooked in coconut milk and served with mango. Yum!

AMAZING MAIZE
Ways to eat corn

Like rice, maize (also known as "corn") is a staple ingredient for people all over the world. That means it's eaten by a lot of people, a lot of the time.

Maize is actually a type of grass, and the large flower that grows at the top is called an "ear." The little bumpy bits that we eat are known as "kernels." They're technically seeds and there are typically more than 600 on every ear!

A particularly popular type of maize is sweetcorn — it's sweet, and yellow, and eaten in many countries. But there are a lot of other varieties and colors, including black, blue, purple, green, red . . . some ears are even MULTICOLORED! So it's no surprise that maize is used to make an amazing number of very different things.

Not just food

Maize isn't just used to feed humans. Most of the maize we grow is actually given to animals. It's also used to make things like fireworks, glue, paint, soap, shoe polish, and plastic — none of which taste very good at all . . .

SWEETCORN

Sweetcorn is eaten in side dishes, salads, soups, and stews. It's also used to make dessert like Vietnamese **CHÈ BẮP** *(chair bap)*, made from coconut milk, sweetcorn, and tapioca pearls (see page 25).

People often cut the kernels off the ear before eating them. But you can also eat the kernels when they're still attached. In Mexico, whole ears of corn called **ELOTES** *(eh-loh-tez)* are skewered onto a stick, covered with mayonnaise, cheese, and chili, and sold as a snack.

POPCORN

Popcorn is a specific type of maize whose kernels, when heated, magically pop, explode, grow, and turn into a light and crispy puff.

CORNMEAL

Some types of maize are dried and ground into corn flour or cornmeal, which looks and feels like coarse flour. People use it to make bread and cakes, like **AREPAS** *(ah-reh-pa)* in Colombia and **BOBOTA** *(bo-boh-ta)* in Greece.

It can also be mixed with water or milk before cooking to make a porridge or wet paste. This is called **POLENTA** *(poh-len-ta)* in Italy, **MĂMĂLIGĂ** *(muh-muh-lee-guh)* in Romania, **NSHIMA** *(in-shi-mah)* in Zambia, **UGALI** *(ooh-gah-lee)* in Kenya, and **COU-COU** *(koo-koo)* in Trinidad and Tobago.

MASA
(mah-sa)

Thousands of years ago, people in Mexico and Guatemala discovered a way of cooking maize that made it softer and easier to digest. That same process is still used today, and the cooked maize is made into thick soups such as **POZOLE** *(po-zoh-lay)* in Mexico or **HOMINY GRITS** in the US.

You can also turn this maize into a flour called **MASA HARINA** *(mah-sa ha-ree-na)*, which is used to make **TORTILLAS** *(tor-tee-yas)* for **TACOS**, **QUESADILLAS** *(keh-sah-dee-yas)*, **TOTOPOS** *(to-to-pos)*, and more.

SYRUP

Corn can be used to make syrups to sweeten cakes, breakfast cereals, candy, and soft drinks. These syrups are used a LOT, partly because they're cheaper than sugar. They're also invisible, but worth looking for on ingredient lists . . . too much syrup isn't very good for you. In fact, over time, it can make you very sick.

BEAUTIFUL BREAD

Bread around the world

The first bread was made nearly 12,000 years ago. Now, bread is enjoyed everywhere — and in some cultures it's eaten with almost every meal. What it looks like, how it's made, and how it tastes varies from country to country.

In Morocco, families often make their own dough at home before carrying it to their local community oven. There, a baker cooks the dough into a soft, flat loaf called MEDINA BREAD (meh-dee-na).

People in France buy fresh bread from their local bakery. BAGUETTES (bag-etts) are particularly popular. These long sticks are light and fluffy on the inside, crisp and crusty on the outside.

LAVASH (la-vash) is a type of bread from Iran, Armenia, Kazakhstan, and Turkey that is extremely thin, floppy, and roughly the same size as a pillowcase. It's used to scoop up herbs and cheese, or is wrapped around meat kebabs.

In countries like Denmark, Norway, and Sweden, bread is often dark or even black because of the dark rye grain that's used to make the flour. A slice of rye bread can be dense, but also moist and sticky. It's often eaten with eggs or smoked fish on top — a snack that's called SMØRREBRØD (smuhr-brud) in Denmark.

There are many, many types of bread in India. ROTI (roh-tee) and PARATHA (pa-rah-ta) are very thin, everyday breads eaten with most meals. They're cooked on top of a hot iron plate called a tawa.

BAGELS (or beigels) were originally made by Jewish people who lived in Poland, but are now eaten around the world. They're unusual because the dough is boiled in water before being baked. They also have a hole in the middle!

What is bread?

Bread is made from a mixture of flour and water called "dough." Sometimes other ingredients are added for flavor or texture, including spices, butter, olive oil, salt, milk, or seeds. Flour can be made from different types of wheat, corn, and even rice. This is one of the reasons why there are so many types of bread.

Another ingredient that can be added is yeast. Yeast is a type of fungi and, when it's mixed with dough and left for a while, it creates air bubbles. This can make bread light and fluffy. Bread that doesn't have yeast in it is usually pretty flat once cooked. This type of bread is called "unleavened."

LUNCH ON THE GO

What's in your packed lunch?

TIFFINS *(ti-fins)* (also known as **DABBA** *(dab-bas)* are Indian lunch boxes made up of three to four round tins that stack on top of each other. They're filled with home-cooked lentils, pickles, spiced vegetables, and rice, and delivered around cities in time for lunch.

You know when it's lunchtime in Norway because you hear the rustling of people unwrapping their **MATPAKKE** *(mart-pah-keh)*. This Norwegian packed lunch consists of buttered bread — with a topping such as meat, cheese, or fish-egg spread — wrapped in stiff, waxed paper.

A popular lunch in South Africa is **BUNNY CHOW**, a small bread loaf that's hollowed out and stuffed with curry. The bread acts as an edible lunch box!

A **DOSIRAK** *(toh-shee-rak)*, or South Korean lunch box, includes meat, cooked rice, and side dishes like seaweed and a hot, tangy cabbage called **KIMCHI** *(kim-chee)*. The box has little dividers to keep the different foods separate while traveling.

Can I try one of each, please?

Many children in England and the US take a packed lunch to school. This often includes **SANDWICHES** — two pieces of bread with a filling in between, like peanut butter and jelly, ham and cheese, or egg salad — as well as some fruit, chips, and yogurt.

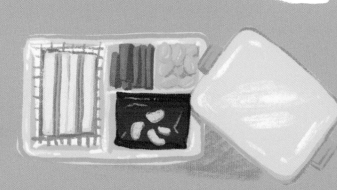

NOODLES, NOODLES

Oodles of noodles

All noodles begin with a simple mix of flour, water, and sometimes eggs. The mix is then poured, flattened, or rolled by machine, hands, or feet!

There are a lot of different ways to turn dough into noodles . . .

Hundreds of years ago in Japan, women started stomping on dough with their feet to make UDON noodles. They even carried backpacks with books to make themselves heavier! It's much easier than using your hands . . .

You can press it down over lots of wires.

You can cut it using a machine.

Or you can push it through a funny-shaped hole.

You can use a knife to chop it into ribbons.

What's in a name?

Although it comes in a wide variety of colors, shapes, and sizes, pasta is basically a type of noodle. There are about 350 different varieties of pasta and most shapes are designed to hold a particular sauce. That's why pasta can be twirly, stringy, square, rounded, hollow, long, short, fat, or thin. And their names usually describe what they look like . . .

ORECCHIETTE
(o-reh-kee-yeh-teh)
means "little ears"
in Italian

FAZZOLETTI
(fa-zzoh-leh-tee)
means "silk handkerchief"

FARFALLE
(far-fah-lay)
means
"butterflies"

LOKSHYNA *(lock-shee-na)* from Ukraine are soft noodles made from flour and eggs. They're often eaten with creamy or buttery sauces.

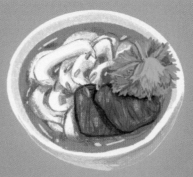

DAO XIAO MIAN *(tau see-ow mee-an)* from Shanxi province, China, are chewy ribbons that have been cut or shaved into water from a block of dough.

SPÄTZLE *(shpetz-el)* are short noodles from Austria. The name means "little sparrows," but you have to look hard to see a resemblance!

Did you know that a bowl of noodles made 4,000 years ago was found in China? It might be the oldest example of noodles!

VERMICELLI *(ver-me-chell-ee)* from Vietnam are pale white threads made from rice flour and water. They're delicious served cooked but cold in a salad.

SPAGHETTI is one of Italy's many shapes of noodle — or "pasta." It's long, thin, and stringy, and can be slurpy to eat!

NUM BANH CHOK *(nom ban jock)* are rice noodles from Cambodia. They're typically eaten for breakfast in a fish and coconut soup that has the same name.

CAVATAPPI *(cav-a-tapp-ee)* means "corkscrew"

LINGUINE *(lin-gwee-nee)* means "little tongues"

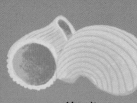

LUMACHE *(loo-mah-kay)* means "snails"

RADIATORE *(ra-dee-a-tor-eh)* means "radiators"

DISCHI VOLANTI *(dish-ee voh-lan-tee)* means "flying saucers"

HOT, HOT, HOT
Chili peppers are HOT!

Did you know that there is an official rating system called the Scoville scale that tells you just how hot they are? Here are some examples of dishes using chilies—from burning to tingling.

SALSA
Mexico is the home of the chili, including the *jalapeño (ha-la-peh-nyoh)*. There are more than 150 types of chilies and Mexicans eat 15 times more per day than northern Europeans. They also eat a lot of salsa — a fresh sauce that often includes tomatoes, onions, and . . . you guessed it . . . CHILIES.

In Mexico, we eat chilies in almost every meal. We roast, stuff, dry, pickle, smoke, and fry them!

SOM TAM
(som tam)
As a Thai salad made from fruit, you might think this would be sweet and refreshing . . . But, in fact, it's SERIOUSLY SPICY, thanks to all the extra fiery small bird's eye chilies dropped in.

NASHVILLE HOT CHICKEN
This dish was created in the US when someone tried to cook an extra-spicy breakfast as revenge. The spiky-hot sauce made from cayenne pepper powder is as tasty as it is toasty and it's now an iconic Nashville dish.

CHONGQING CHICKEN
(chong-chii-ung)
Although the title would suggest that chicken is the main ingredient in this Chinese dish, there are actually more dried Sichuan red chilies than meat!

SCOTCH BONNET SAUCE
In some Caribbean islands, this is more popular than ketchup. It's always on the table at mealtimes! It's very, very, VERY hot — that's because Scotch bonnet is one of the hottest chillies around.

The Scoville scale is used to measure how spicy a chilli is. They are measured in "Scoville Heat Units" (SHU).

JALAPEÑO
4,000–8,500 Scovilles

CAYENNE PEPPER
30,000–50,000 Scovilles

BIRD'S-EYE THAI CHILI
50,000–100,000 Scovilles

SCOTCH BONNET
100,000–350,000 Scovilles

CAROLINA REAPER
1,500,000–2,200,000 Scovilles!

TERRIFIC TOMATOES

Did you know there are 10,000 types of tomato?

They're not just red and round . . . some are yellow, black, green, pink, purple, pointy, lumpy, and long!

More than 650 million bottles and 11 billion packets of **KETCHUP** are sold in over 140 countries each year!

XI HONG SHI CHAO JI DAN (*see ho-ung schuh chow chi tan*) is a mix of eggs and tomatoes and is one of the most eaten dishes in China. And it has the same colors as the Chinese flag!

Bake eggs in a spiced tomato sauce to make **SHAKSHOUKA** (*shak-shoo-ka*), a popular breakfast dish from North Africa and the Middle East. Yum!

SALMOREJO (*sal-mor-egh-ho*) is a cold Spanish soup made of blended tomatoes and bread — it's shiny, thick, and creamy.

PANZANELLA (*pan-za-nell-a*) is an Italian salad made with lots of tomatoes, stale bread, olive oil, and many other DELICIOUS things.

IS IT A FRUIT?

A fruit is anything we eat that has a seed. For example, peaches, pears, and plums.

That means that some things we think of as vegetables are actually fruits, including tomatoes, chilies, eggplants, pumpkins, bean pods, and peas!

But even though tomatoes and chilies are, technically speaking, fruits, its fine to call them vegetables when you're cooking.

DO YOU DIG IT?

Potatoes, cassavas, and yams

Some of the most nutritious things that humans eat are hard, lumpy, and grow underground. Potatoes, sweet potatoes, cassavas, and yams are all kinds of "tubers," which develop on stems and roots as a way for plants to store energy so that they can regrow the next year.

POTATOES

The potato originally comes from Peru, but it's grown and eaten around the world.

Potatoes are the world's third most eaten ingredient.

More than a BILLION people eat potatoes — that's one in every six of us.

Almost ten times more potatoes are grown than carrots — the weight of one million jumbo jets a year!

The largest potato ever grown weighed just under 9 pounds — about the size of a newborn baby!

YAMS

Yams can be white, yellow, and even purple!

Like potatoes, they tend to be boiled, mashed, baked, or fried to eat as fries or chips. They're also used to make dumplings and cakes.

Yams are eaten all over the world — including countries in Southeast Asia and the Caribbean — but they're a particularly important food for African countries such as Nigeria, Ghana, Ivory Coast, and Benin.

CASSAVAS

Cassavas are one of the most important vegetables in the world. They're useful because they can grow in hot, dry climates and last a long time once harvested.

Cassavas are also known as MANIOC (mah-nee-ock) or YUCA (yuh-kuh).

Cassavas MUST be soaked for days before being cooked, otherwise they can make you sick.

In West and Central Africa, cassava is turned into a doughy paste called FUFU (foo-foo). It's usually eaten with soups and stews.

Sometimes cassava is cooked, dried, and turned into a type of flour called TAPIOCA (ta-pee-oh-ka). In Taiwan, tapioca is used to make all sorts of things, like dumpling wrappers, porridge, and boba—the chewy balls used in drinks and desserts.

There are more than 5,000 types of potato! They're used to make all kinds of dishes, including:

Tiny potato dumplings from Italy called GNOCCHI (nyo-ckee). They are soft and bouncy and usually eaten with a buttery, cheesy sauce.

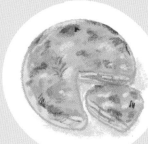

TORTILLA DE PATATAS (tor-tee-ya de pa-ta-tas) from Spain — a mix of sliced potatoes, onions, and beaten eggs. They're fried in a pan until firm and golden.

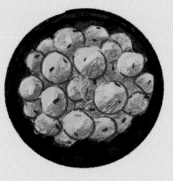

JEERA ALOO (jee-ruh aa-loo) from northern India — made from boiled potatoes fried with LOTS of spices.

Thin, shredded-potato pancakes called GAMJA-JEON (gam-ja-jurn) from South Korea. They're eaten with a dipping sauce, made from soy sauce and vinegar.

POTATO RÖSTI (rur-stee) is one of Switzerland's national dishes. It's SO well-loved that it can be eaten for breakfast, lunch, or dinner!

EAT YOUR GREENS

Vegetables around the world

Green vegetables (particularly the leafy ones) are packed with nutrients and this makes them a very important part of our diet. We also eat them because they're DELICIOUS! Here are some glorious greens from all over the world.

Furry little **OKRA** *(o-kra)* pods are also known as "ladies fingers" and are common in African, Indian, and Sri Lankan food, as well as in the Southern US. Okra can be slimy when you cook or cut it . . . but don't let that keep you from trying it!

Cabbage is eaten all over the world. One type that's popular in northern Europe is **POINTED CABBAGE**. It's known as "sweetheart" or "hispi," and grows in a cone shape.

CHOY SUM has a crunchy stem and tiny yellow flowers. It's especially popular in Southeast Asia and China.

ROMANESCO *(row-man-ess-ko)* **BROCCOLI** is originally from Italy. It's about the same size as your head and its florets are spiraling, bright green, and pointy.

ARTICHOKE is common in Italy and France, and is the bud of a plant called a thistle. Peel off the furry middle and woody leaves, and you'll reach a soft inside called the "heart."

I love SNAKE BEANS! In the Philippines, we typically chop them up because they're very long —that's why some people call them "yardlong!"

The thick and sturdy stems of a **JUTE** *(joot)* **MALLOW** plant can grow twice as tall as humans! In Egypt, the leaves are known as **MOLOKHIA** *(mloh-khee-ah)* or "vegetable for kings" because they were made into a soup for pharaohs to eat when they were sick.

CHARD (also known as "silverbeet") is a leafy vegetable that's grown and gobbled across northern Europe and Oceania. It has an earthy taste and yellow, white, or bright red stalks.

BITTER MELON is grown in Africa and Asia. The flesh is crunchy and watery like a cucumber and the outside is very, VERY bumpy.

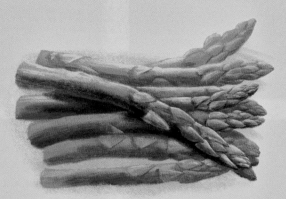

ASPARAGUS is really popular in European countries like the UK and Germany. The finger-thick spears taste fresh and grassy. But, be warned: eating a lot of them can make your pee turn green and smelly!

Peas are sweet little seeds that grow in pods and POP in your mouth. There's one type of pea where you don't just eat the seed, you eat the pod it grows in too. It's called **MANGE-TOUT** *(monj-too)*, which is French and means "eat everything."

PICKLES AND FERMENTS

Do you know what sour tastes like?

If you're not sure what sour is, try nibbling on a slice of lemon or taking a sip of vinegar . . . Sour food can make you wince — which sounds bad, but lots of people actually enjoy it.

One popular way to make sour food is "pickling." Humans have been doing this for thousands of years because it makes the ingredients and the good things in them (their "nutrients") last longer. This means there's something to eat during the times of year when it's harder to grow food.

Pickling makes food last longer by making it very acidic — this means bad bacteria don't grow. The acid doesn't just preserve the food, it also makes it taste deliciously sour!

Ingredients like fruits and vegetables can be pickled in two ways. They might be soaked in vinegar (which is very acidic) or they might be "fermented." Fermenting encourages tiny organisms, including good bacteria that are already in foods, to "eat" that food and create acid. The bad bacteria hate this and stay away!

PICKLES

TSUKEMONO *(tsoo-kay-moh-no)* means "pickled things" in Japanese. Classic ingredients include ginger *(gari)*, a radish called "daikon" *(takuan)*, plums *(umeboshi)*, and cucumbers *(kyurizuke)*. They're eaten with almost every meal.

In Ukraine, we sometimes grow so many WATERMELONS in the summer, the only way to make sure they're not wasted is to pickle them!

We put them in big barrels of salty water and herbs and wait for them to turn sour.

Some pickles are not just sour, they're sweet and spicy too. To make **ACAR** *(atch-ah)*, fruits and vegetables such as carrots, cucumbers, green beans, and pineapple are coated with a paste that contains spices, dried shrimp, sugar, and vinegar. Acar is eaten with many Malaysian and Indonesian meals.

You'll find **KIMCHI** *(kim-chee)* in pretty much every South Korean home, and served at most meals. A lot of different vegetables can be used, but most of the time it's made from fermented cabbage or radish. Chili flakes often turn the kimchi hot and red.

SAUERKRAUT *(sour-krout)* means "sour cabbage" in German — and that's what it is: lots of finely sliced white cabbage that's left to ferment and turn sour. It's not just eaten in Germany. Many countries in Central Europe — like Poland, Romania, Czech Republic, and Slovakia — are also huge fans.

There are many different kinds of pickled and fermented cucumbers. Big, bumpy, crunchy, and crispy cucumbers are pickled with dill in Eastern Europe. Sliced pickled cucumbers are eaten inside burgers or alongside sandwiches in the US. And in France, tiny little cucumbers, or "pickles," called **CORNICHONS** *(cor-nee-shon)* are often eaten with cold meats.

Which pickles would you pick?

VEGETABLE DISHES
How do you eat yours?

Some children are vegetarians and don't eat meat or fish at all. There are many reasons for that, including worries about the way animals are treated and the potential impact on the environment. Another reason is religion. In Jainism, everyone is a vegetarian, and so are many Buddhists, Hindus, and Sikhs. Because there are so many vegetables and so much that can be made from them, you can see why vegetarians don't feel like they're missing out! Which of these dishes have you tried?

RICE AND CURRY
Sri Lanka's national dish doesn't come with just one curry. It contains an array of them and some are packed with brightly colored vegetables like pumpkins, beets, and jackfruit.

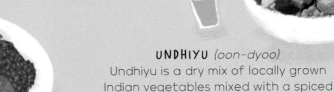

UNDHIYU *(oon-dyoo)*
Undhiyu is a dry mix of locally grown Indian vegetables mixed with a spiced paste and cooked upside down underneath hot pots.

YETSOM BEYAYNETU and NAI TSOM MIGBI
For people in Ethiopia and Eritrea, vegetables are a key part of their diet. That's because they often don't eat meat for religious reasons. These traditional vegetable dishes are made up of different stews served on a spongy pancake called **INJERA** *(in-jeh-rah)*.

ALLOCO *(all-oh-ko)*
Chunks of plantain with a feisty red-pepper sauce are BIG in Ivory Coast. They're served alongside many meals. And, in bustling towns and cities, they're also enjoyed on their own as a snack.

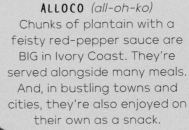

GADO GADO *(ga-doe ga-doe)*
To make this Indonesian salad, mix crunchy vegetables with eggs and tofu. Then add LOTS of sweet-salty-hot peanut dressing.

Gado gado is my favorite— and it means "mix mix!"

PEPPER POT SOUP
This Jamaican soup is made from yams and a leafy green vegetable called *callaloo* *(cah-lah-loo)*. It also has Scotch bonnet chilies, which makes it fiery hot!

POTATO SALAD
This is a popular dish all over Germany. Different regions make potato salad in different ways, but they're often served with the local *wurst* (sausages).

DOLMA *(doll-ma)*
In Turkish, dolma means "stuffed!" All kinds of vegetables are stuffed—from peppers to tomatoes, cabbages to zucchini. They're crammed with veggies, rice, and meat, and packed tightly together before being cooked until they are shiny, soft, and scrumptious.

BORSCHT *(borsh)*
The stars of this Eastern European soup are the vegetables. They vary depending on what's grown locally and what's in season, but might include purple or orange beets, cabbage, onions, and tomatoes.

HELLO, HERBS
Flavorful plants

Herbs are a type of plant whose leaves are used to add flavor to food. They usually smell amazing! Some are hard and best when cooked, others are soft and best when added to food at the last minute. But whether they're fresh or fried, chopped or whole, herbs give an explosion of flavor and can change how food looks, smells, and tastes.

Like many Vietnamese dishes, **PHỞ** *(fuh)* is served with a separate plate of garnishes. This usually includes big handfuls of holy basil, shiso, culantro, and mint. When mixed into the noodle soup, their minty-fresh flavors rush up your nose.

The Scandinavian salmon dish **GRAVLAKS** *(grav-lucks)* was originally made by burying fish in sand! Nowadays, the salmon is left for a day or two under salt, sugar, and lots and lots of dill. It's then thinly sliced and served with a mustard and dill sauce.

SHISO

BASIL

THYME

SAGE

In France, herbs are often added to soups and stews to give them flavor. They're tied up in a bunch so that you can easily take them out when it's time to eat. The tasty bundle is called a **BOUQUET GARNI** *(boo-kay gar-nee)* and can include herbs like rosemary, tarragon, savory, sage, parsley, or thyme. If the herbs are dry instead of fresh, they're often kept in a little bag so the flavors (but not the herbs) can escape.

The Iranian dish **KUKU SABZI** *(koo-koo sab-zee)* is made by whisking eggs and adding lots and lots of chopped herbs like cilantro, fenugreek, parsley, and dill. The runny liquid is then cooked in a shallow pan until it becomes firm. Because there are so many herbs in the dish, it's completely green! It's usually served when celebrating a festival called *Nowruz* (or Persian New Year) because the herbs symbolize new life.

Italian **PESTO** is made from big bunches of fresh basil, pine nuts, and salt. The ingredients are added to a special bowl called a "mortar" and pounded with a blunt stick called a "pestle." They're then mixed with olive oil and a cheese called *Parmigiano-Reggiano (par-mi-jaa-no-reh-jaa-no)* to make the perfect sauce for pasta.

DILL

ROSEMARY

FENUGREEK

A SPRINKLE OF SPICE

Tastes like home

Spices can be roots, seeds, flowers, or fruits. They're typically dried so that they last longer. They're then ground into a powder or soaked in water. Spices are used to season and change the flavor, smell, and sometimes even color of food. They bring dishes to life and are often what makes something taste like home.

As well as being used on their own, spices can be mixed together. These blends are unique to particular cuisines, countries, and regions. Some spice blends are vital when making national dishes, while others are an optional seasoning.

The impact spice blends have is amazing — here are a few you might like to try.

ZA'ATAR *(za-tar)* is a spice mix from the Middle East that includes dried herbs like thyme and oregano, plus sesame seeds, and a zingy powder from the sumac berry. Za'atar is rubbed on meat and fish, added to stews, and sprinkled over bread and salads.

There are seven ingredients in **SHICHIMI TŌGARASHI** *(shi-chi-mee toe-ga-rash-ee).* This hot Japanese blend includes sesame and poppy seeds, dried seaweed, fiery ground chili and sanshō peppers, and a splash of sour from dried orange or yuzu peel. So much flavor! It's often sprinkled on noodles, warm rice, or raw fish.

ADVIEH *(ad-vee-yeh)* means "spice" and is used in Iran to add a floral fragrance to rice dishes and stews. It includes sweet spices such as cinnamon, turmeric, cardamom, cloves, and rose petals.

ZA'ATAR

SHICHIMI TŌGARASHI

ADVIEH

Can we get some ADVIEH? I like sprinkling that on rice pudding!

KHMELI SUNELI *(kh-mel-ee soo-nel-ee)* literally means "spice" and is the national spice blend of the country of Georgia. It includes the dried leaves of the marigold flower, dried herbs such as basil, dill, parsley, mint, and musty blue fenugreek seeds. It's used to season a lot of different foods, including beans and roast vegetables.

BERBERE *(ber-buh-ray)* includes spices such as dried chilies, ginger, cilantro, and paprika. It gives food a deep, warm flavor and is used in many Ethiopian dishes.

Which of these spice blends would you like to try?

KHMELI SUNELI

BERBERE

YAJI

YAJI *(yaa-jee)* is a fiery, nutty blend of spices, full of different-colored peppercorns, ground peanuts, and chili flakes. It's an essential part of a dish called **SUYA** *(soo-ya)* from Ghana and Nigeria, which is made by coating pieces of beef, chicken, or goat in the spices and threading them onto a stick.

QUATRE ÉPICES *(cat-ruh eh-pis)* is a blend of four spices: white pepper, ginger, cloves, and nutmeg. It's often used to season traditional French meat dishes such as **PÂTÉS** *(pa-tay)* and **TERRINES** *(teh-reen)*.

QUATRE ÉPICES

PANCH PHORAN

RAS EL HANOUT

In Arabic, **RAS EL HANOUT** *(rahs el han-oot)* means "head of the shop." That's because this spice blend from Egypt is a luxurious mix of the best spices the seller has to offer. There are often at least 12 different spices in the mix, and the sunset-colored blend usually includes paprika, cumin, nutmeg, allspice, mace, and more.

Used in East India and Bangladesh, **PANCH PHORAN** *(panch for-an)* is a mix of five spices: cumin, brown mustard, fenugreek, nigella, and fennel seeds. But the seeds are not ground—instead, they're often fried in oil until they POP!

I want the one with yellow flowers in it!

35

POPPED FROM A POD

From borlotti beans to black-eyed peas

Pulses are little seeds that grow in pods on a special type of plant (known as "legumes"). They're full of things we need to stay healthy—like protein, vitamins, fiber, and carbohydrates. And they're an important food across the world.

Do you recognize any of these?

BUTTER BEANS

CHICKPEAS

RED LENTILS

FAVA BEANS

MUNG BEANS

There can be MILLIONS of seeds in just one field and each one has to be shaken out of its pod!

BLACK-EYED PEAS

BORLOTTI BEANS

CARLIN PEAS

In some West African countries, **BLACK-EYED PEAS** are so popular that people eat them every day. In Ghana, they're mixed with lots of red ingredients like tomatoes, palm oil, and chili peppers. They're served with fried plantains, which are also red—and that's why the dish is called **RED-RED**.

In India, **LENTILS**—and the dishes made from them—are called **DAL** (daal). They're a very important part of Indian cuisine and come in many different colors, including red, yellow, and green. **DAL MAKHANI** (daal muk-nee) is a rich, smoky dish where black lentils are cooked for hours and hours over coals.

FALAFEL (fa-la-fel) is a popular dish from Egypt, Israel, and Palestine. It's made from **CHICKPEAS** or **FAVA BEANS** that are ground, spiced, and shaped into discs before being deep-fried. They're often stuffed into the warm and fluffy pockets of a bread called **PITA**, along with crunchy salad and hot, nutty sauces. YUM!

SOYBEANS

Multitalented beans

Soybeans are originally from China, Japan, and Korea. These pulses can be cooked when fresh and still in their pods. But they can also be preserved, fermented, and turned into things that look nothing like a bean!

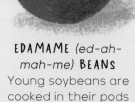

EDAMAME *(ed-ah-mah-me)* **BEANS**
Young soybeans are cooked in their pods and eaten as a green vegetable.

SOY SAUCE
Soybeans are fermented before being turned into a paste and finally into a liquid.

TOFU *(toe-foo)*
Soy milk that's been turned into a solid block: it can be firm and spongy, or silky and soft.

DOUCHI
(doe-chee)
Black beans that are fermented, salted, and used to add flavor to a dish.

MISO *(me-so)* and **DOENJANG** *(dwen-jang)*
A sweet and salty paste that can take up to three years to make!

NUTS

Nuts about nuts!

Nuts are seeds that grow inside hard shells on plants and trees. They're used as ingredients — sometimes whole, sometimes chopped, and sometimes ground as fine as flour.

As well as being used for cooking, nuts make excellent snacks and can be eaten raw, roasted, or toasted.

I'm from Syria, and my favorite treat is SWAR AS-SITT. It means "lady's bracelet," but I think my wrist would get very sticky if I wore it!

ALMOND

MACADAMIA

PISTACHIO

CASHEW

HAZELNUT

WALNUT

BRAZIL

BEAUTIFUL BEEF

From head to tail

Cows are BIG! The ones that humans eat tend to weigh 1,212 – 1,410 pounds. That's heavier than a grand piano!

Because it's such an enormous animal, different parts of a cow are used to make different types of dishes. Some "cuts" of beef are best cooked for a really long time, some for a few moments, and some not at all!

Here are just a few of the ways that the different parts of a cow are used all over the world.

Animal stomachs are lined with something called "tripe." It has an amazing honeycomb texture and, if carefully cleaned and cooked, is soft and jiggly. One of Ecuador's national dishes is a tripe stew called **GUATITA** *(gwa-tee-ta).*

The prime rib section of a cow contains seven large ribs . . . that's a lot of meat! In countries such as the UK and US, this hefty piece of cow tends to be divided by the bone and roasted in an oven for a special occasion.

In Indonesia, very few parts of the cow go to waste and even the hide (skin) of a cow is eaten. **RAMBAK PETIS** *(rum-bahk puh-tiz)* is deep-fried cow hide coated in a funky sweet and spicy paste.

OSSOBUCO *(oss-oh-boo-ko),* or "bone with a hole," is a classic Italian dish where round steaks are cut from a cow's front leg — the "shin." It's cooked until very soft and often served with a creamy, golden risotto.

A cow's tail has a surprising amount of meat and flavor. In the classic Jamaican dish, **BROWN OXTAIL STEW**, chunks of tail are stewed with scotch bonnet peppers and butter beans.

Brisket, skirt, and flank steaks come from the chest and belly of a cow. They're very tough, but cooking them gently for a long time means the meat becomes so soft and juicy that you can pull it apart with spoons, forks, or fingers. This is how to cook the flank steak in ROPA VIEJA *(roh-pa vee-eh-ya)*, a Cuban dish that literally means "old clothes!"

Many countries have traditional dishes made from cow brains — for example, the Colombian dish TARTA DE SESO *(tar-ta de say-so)*, which is a creamy pie filled with spinach, cheese, and brains.

Short ribs are cut from the chest section of a cow's ribcage. The Brazilian stew VACA ATOLADA *(va-ka a-toh-la-da)* means "cow stuck in the mud!" That's because the ribs cook for a long time, until you're left with soft pieces of beef in a thick, sticky gravy.

The fillet is a very tender piece of beef. In the British dish BEEF WELLINGTON, fillet is wrapped in a meaty spread called PÂTÉ *(pa-tay)*, finely chopped mushrooms, and puff pastry.

Beef bones carry a LOT of flavor, so people across the world boil them to make stocks and broths for soups, for example SEOLLEONGTANG *(suh-long-tang)* from South Korea.

Meat from the back legs of cows can be salted, cured, and dried for a long time. In the Spanish delicacy CECINA *(cheh-chee-na)*, it's then cut very thinly and eaten like ham.

Chuck meat comes from the shoulder and has just the right amount of fat to be ground up and made into HAMBURGERS. In case you were wondering, the hamburger is made of beef, not ham, and is named after the German city of Hamburg.

The insides of a cow, including organs like their liver, kidneys, tongue, brain, and heart, are called "offcuts" or "offal." In China, thin slices of tongue, heart, and other types of offal are coated in mouth-numbing spices to create the dish FUQI FEIPIAN *(foo-chee fay-pee-an)*.

BILLIONS OF BIRDS

Which do you prefer, chicken or egg?

More than one third of all the meat that humans eat is poultry — or birds.
And most of those birds are chickens. People eat a lot of them,
a mind-boggling 70 billion each year!

Originally, people ate chicken because these small animals could be kept by most families. Now, they're farmed on a much, MUCH bigger scale. Chicken goes well with so many different flavors. It can also be cooked in a variety of ways. That's why it's so popular across the world.

DEEP-FRIED
To "deep-fry" chicken, coat it in a sticky, drippy batter and cook in crazy-hot oil. This works especially well with chicken thighs and legs (or "drumsticks"). The result is mouth-watering meat with a crunchy shell. People in the US, Japan, Korea, Thailand, and many more countries cook chicken this way.

POACHED
Sometimes pieces of chicken (or the entire bird!) are cooked gently in hot water. This is called "poaching." One of Singapore's national dishes is CHICKEN RICE, where a whole chicken is dunked in and out of a pot until it's tender and juicy. It's sliced and served with cucumber, sauces, and rice.

BRAISED
Many chicken dishes are "braised" or "stewed." This means cooking the meat with a tasty liquid, which becomes the scrumptious sauce. And it's this sauce that makes the dish well-known.

In the Philippines, people cook chicken in lots of vinegar and soy sauce to make CHICKEN ADOBO. And in Senegal, children enjoy YASSA AU POULET (yass-ah oh poo-lay) with its sweet and tangy sauce full of onions and lemons.

BARBECUED
Humans love cooking chicken over fire! This is called "grilling" or "barbecuing." The smoky flavor is an important part of dishes like PERI PERI CHICKEN from Mozambique and Portugal, and JERK CHICKEN from Jamaica, which is cooked over the branches and leaves of the pimento tree.

Excellent eggs

On average, each human eats around 180 chicken eggs a year! We eat them on their own (boiled, fried, scrambled, poached), but also as ingredients in things like cakes and meringues. And some countries eat more than others. For example, in Mexico, people eat around 370 a year (more than one a day), whereas in South Africa, the number is more like 120.

Other birds lay eggs you can eat too. One of the main differences between them is their size:

CHICKENS lay the classic egg!

QUAILS lay tiny eggs that look like stones.

PHEASANT eggs are about half the size of chicken eggs, and green-gray in color. They have a rich flavor and a deep-yellow yolk.

TURKEY eggs are similar in size to duck eggs, but with a speckled cream shell. And lots and LOTS of yolk!

DUCK eggs are a bit bigger than chicken eggs — their shells are usually white or pale blue.

GOOSE eggs are usually white and delicious when scrambled. They're roughly the size of an adult human's palm.

These blue and green speckled **EMU** eggs are each about the same size as 12 chicken eggs.

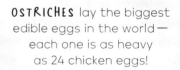

OSTRICHES lay the biggest edible eggs in the world — each one is as heavy as 24 chicken eggs!

More and more chickens

One reason we eat so much chicken is that, over the last 60 years, humans have figured out how to grow them very quickly. A chicken that grows naturally and wanders freely takes more than 80 days to reach its full size. A factory-farmed chicken, on the other hand, takes 42 days, or sometimes even less. These chickens don't get to roam around. Instead, they're usually kept in very cramped conditions. They are also given foods that make them put on weight fast, and are pumped full of medication called "antibiotics" to stop them from getting sick. These antibiotics make it into the meat we eventually eat, which isn't very good for us.

This doesn't mean we shouldn't eat chicken at all. But should we eat quite so much?

PORK, GLORIOUS PORK

Pulled, roasted, dried, or stewed

Of all the different types of meat, pork is the one humans eat most of. It's particularly popular in China, where around two thirds of all pork is eaten.

Pork can be roasted in big pieces, cooked as smaller chops, turned into fresh sausages, or covered in breadcrumbs and fried. But one of the reasons it's eaten by so many people is that it can be preserved to last a very long time. This was very useful before fridges were invented!

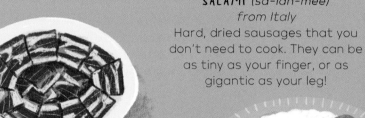

SALAMI *(sa-lah-mee)*
from Italy
Hard, dried sausages that you don't need to cook. They can be as tiny as your finger, or as gigantic as your leg!

PIHTIJIE *(feet-yuh)*
from Serbia
Pieces of meat from all over the pig's body, including the head, are cooked and then left to set like a jelly.

JAMÓN *(ha-mon)*
from Spain
Whole pig legs are packed in salt, washed, and then dried for at least a year before being very thinly sliced.

SALTED PIG TAILS
from Jamaica
Used to add flavor to hearty bean stews.

SALO *(sa-loh)*
from Ukraine
Looks like cheese, but it's actually the cold white fat from a pig's back!

ROUSONG *(row so-ung)*
from China
Pork that is cooked, shredded, and fried until fluffy and light, like cotton candy.

BLODPUDDING
from Sweden
Pig blood mixed with seasoning, flour, butter, and beer.

SOUSE *(sowse)*
from Antigua and Trinidad and Tobago
Meat from pig feet, cooked, pickled, and served in a broth.

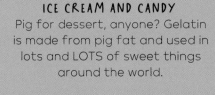

ICE CREAM AND CANDY
Pig for dessert, anyone? Gelatin is made from pig fat and used in lots and LOTS of sweet things around the world.

Although it's popular, not everyone eats pork.

Jewish and Muslim children don't eat it for religious reasons.

HUNGRY FOR HANGI
Lamb dishes around the world

The meat from sheep can be called lamb, hogget, or mutton, depending on the age of the animal. In some countries, people barely eat any sheep. But, in others, it's very popular — in Mongolia, people eat on average over 90 pounds a year!

HANGI *(haung-ee)*
In New Zealand, the Māori people use wet cloth or leaves to wrap up lamb, sweet potatoes, potatoes, and cabbage. To cook it, they then bury it underground with very hot rocks.

CHOPAN KABOBS *(chop-pan ka-bobs)*
Across the world, lamb meat is pressed onto skewers, lightly spiced, and cooked over hot coals. One example is *teka kabobs* from Afghanistan — meaty, smoky, and scrumptious.

ASADO *(a-sah-do)*
In Argentina, whole lambs are cut open, attached to crosses, and cooked over firepits or hot coals. The lamb is often served with an herby sauce called *chimichurri (chi-mee-chur-ee)*.

WHOLE SPIT-ROAST LAMB
In many Christian countries such as Greece, lamb is eaten during Easter celebrations. It's often hung on a long metal pole and turned above a fire.

MUTTON HOT POT
Hot pot is an ancient meal where people sit around a pot (which is hot) and cook ingredients for themselves. In Mongolia, an important part of the meal are platters of lamb. They're very thinly sliced, so they cook quickly when dipped in the hot liquid.

QUOZI *(koo-zee)*
A traditional wedding and birthday feast in Iraq often involves a whole lamb stuffed with vegetables, currants, spices, nuts, and . . . even more lamb! It's served on mountains of sweet, spiced rice.

UNDER THE SEA
Shellfish, mollusks and cephalopods

Seafood is some of the most prized food . . . even though it can have hard, stone-like shells, spindly legs, antennae, sharp, pointy claws, or bulbous heads and stringy tentacles! Here are just a few of the weird, wonderful, but very edible, creatures found in the sea.

KING CRAB

LOBSTER

SHELLFISH do have shells, but they aren't actually fish! Confused? Shellfish is really just a word that's used to describe a "crustacean." A crustacean has its skeleton and hard shell on the outside of its body and usually lives in water.

BLUE CRAB

BROWN CRAB

PRAWN AND SHRIMP

Seafood dishes

DEEP-FRIED SOFT-SHELL CRABS
Many countries fry crabs that have soft shells. They're soft because the crabs have just outgrown and shed their old, harder shell. This means you can eat everything — body, legs, and claws! In Vietnam, CUA LỘT CHIÊN GIÒN (cour lot chia john) is made from crabs that are deep-fried until they're crisp on the outside and soft and juicy on the inside. They're eaten with a salty, fragrant dipping sauce.

ALASKAN KING CRAB LEGS
The only edible part of a king crab is the meat in its bumpy, hard-shelled, and very long legs. These crabs are so big that one leg usually weighs at least one pound — the weight of a soccer ball! The sweet meat is usually cooked and eaten very simply, often with nothing more than butter and lemon.

RAZOR CLAMS

WHELKS

ABELONE

RAZOR CLAMS

MOLLUSKS are similar to crustaceans. They have a shell, but no skeleton.

OYSTERS

MUSSELS

OCTOPUS

And then there are CEPHALOPODS. These are a type of mollusk with a big head and lots of tentacles . . . but no shell.

CUTTLEFISH

SQUID

In Greece, we love eating OCTOPUS TENTACLES! We cook them for a long time so they're not too chewy.

OYSTERS
Oysters are often slurped straight from their shells without being cooked. But there are many examples of cooked oysters too. In Singapore, a classic street-food dish is oysters and eggs cooked into an omelet.

MUSSELS
MOULES FRITES (mool freet) is one of Belgium's national dishes — it's a big pot of mussels that have been cooked until the shells pop open. They're eaten with thin french fries and mayonnaise for dipping.

FABULOUS FISH

The most fished fish

On average, humans eat around 44 pounds of fish per person every year. That's the weight of 11 bags of sugar! This means that both the sea and the fish that swim in it are an essential resource — and one that the whole world shares.

ANCHOVIES

These small, "silver," fast-moving fish swim in large, shimmering groups called "schools." Schools sometimes contain hundreds of millions of anchovies! And around 6,613,867 tons are caught every year.

Anchovies have a very strong flavor and are popular across the globe. In Malaysia, they're fried and eaten with breakfast. In Vietnam, they're used to make fish sauce. And in Italy, they're enjoyed on pizza.

SALMON

Salmon is very popular in northern Europe and the US. The pink and juicy flesh can be eaten raw, smoked, steamed, fried, and more, so it's used in many different types of meals.

Most salmon isn't wild, but is instead farmed in nets and cages in the sea. At the moment, this process is not growing healthy fish. It also damages the local environment.

Hopefully, humans will find better ways of farming fish — and also try to eat a greater variety of them.

COD AND POLLOCK

Cod and pollock swim in the Pacific Ocean and North Atlantic Sea. When cooked, they have firm and flaky white flesh. In many countries, they're fried until they're crispy and golden.

Cod is also salted and dried. This means it can last a long time and be transported to different countries without having to keep it cool.

TUNA

More tuna is eaten each year than any other fish. Tuna are large, fast, and silver on the outside, red on the inside. They're important in a lot of cuisines, especially in countries like Spain, Portugal, and the Maldives, where the fish are caught nearby. But the biggest market is Japan, where one quarter of all tuna is eaten, mostly raw.

Overfishing

More fish are caught each year than are being born. This is happening because, instead of fishermen on small boats making short trips to catch fish, humans are using enormous ships and gigantic nets to catch huge amounts.

If humans keep doing this, certain fish will die out. Not only does this mean we won't be able to eat them any more, but the balance of the ocean will change — which is bad for all creatures, both in and out of the sea.

When big fishing nets are used, many fish that aren't supposed to be caught get trapped. For example, when fishing for tuna, dolphins often get trapped in the nets too. Some say that nearly half of the fish caught every year are thrown back overboard because they weren't supposed to be hauled in. Many of them die in the process.

This doesn't mean we shouldn't eat fish at all. Many communities around the world will always rely on fishing on a small scale. But, as with any food, it's important to think about what we eat, where it comes from, and how often we eat it. And, if possible, buy fish that we know has been fished in a way that is responsible and sustainable.

THE MAGIC OF MILK
And the marvelous things we make from it

Milk is a nutritious liquid made by moms — whether that mom is human or animal. Their bodies produce it in order to feed their children, but humans have learned to encourage animals to make extra milk and collect it from them before it gets to their babies. That is how milk is made!

More than six billion people drink animal **MILK** — or eat food that is made from it. These foods include **YOGURT, ICE CREAM, BUTTER, KEFIR, CREAM,** and **CHEESE.** Almost all of these are made from cow's milk, but humans also eat, drink, and make food from the milk of buffalo, horses, reindeer, camels, goats, and sheep.

YOGURT and **KEFIR** *(kef-ear)* are thick, smooth, and taste slightly tangy. They are made by adding bacteria to milk, which makes it ferment (see page 28) and thicken.

Non-dairy milk

In some places, for example Africa and Southeast Asia, people hardly ever drink milk, or eat anything made from it. But they do drink "milk" made from all kinds of other ingredients.

I'm from Singapore and my favorite dessert is made from soy milk. It's called TAU HUAY *(tau hoo-ay)* **and it jiggles!**

In the 1990s, **OAT MILK** was developed in Sweden for people who couldn't, or didn't want to, drink animal milk. To make it, oats are soaked in water then blended together to make a liquid.

If you soak nuts in water then blend them into a liquid, you will get something that looks like milk but tastes like nuts! In Sicily, Italy, a glass of cold **ALMOND MILK** is a classic and refreshing summer drink.

SOY MILK has been around for centuries and is made from soybeans that have been soaked and blended. It tastes and feels very similar to cow's milk. It can also be used to make products like yogurt, cream, and desserts.

I love how butter melts on hot toast!

When milk is left to rest, the fatty milk (or **CREAM**) rises to the top and can be skimmed off. The more fatty the milk, the more luxurious the cream.

If you shake or whisk cream enough, it will turn into **BUTTER**! You'll also be left with a liquid called **BUTTERMILK**, which you can use to make bread and pancakes.

To make **COCONUT MILK**, soak freshly grated coconut flesh in hot water, then blend it into a thick, silky liquid. It's often used as a cooking ingredient in countries where coconuts are grown like Sri Lanka, Indonesia, Papua New Guinea, and Thailand.

RICE MILK is a cloudy, rice-flavored water. Children in Mexico drink **HORCHATA DE ARROZ** *(or-cha-ta de ah-roz)* — a cooling, sweet, milky-white drink made with rice, water, sugar, and cinnamon.

Say cheese!

There are many different types of cheese, with over 1,500 in France alone! They all begin in the same way — by adding bacteria or acid to milk. This turns the milk sour and separates it into liquid and solid parts. And it's the solid parts that are used to make cheese.

Some cheeses are ready almost right away. For example, **MATÓ** *(ma-toh)*, a soft, unsalted cheese from Catalonia, Spain. It's often eaten as a dessert, drizzled with honey.

Some cheeses take a little longer to mature, just long enough for white mold to grow on the outside. This is called the "rind." **CAMEMBERT** *(kam-uhm-bair)* takes three to five weeks to ripen and is soft and creamy on the inside. It can only be made using the milk from cows from a region of France called Normandy.

Some cheeses take even longer. The Swiss cheese **SCHLOSSBERGER** *(shloss-bur-ger)* spends almost two years in caves next to the ruins of a castle before it's ready to eat!

Finally, there are the hard, crumbly cheeses. **PARMIGIANO-REGGIANO** *(par-mi-jaa-no-reh-jaa-no)*, or "Parmesan," from Italy can take up to three years to mature. The average wheel of Parmesan weighs 83.77 pounds — that's heavier than a giant anteater!

ICE CREAM, ICE CREAM

Who wants ice cream?

Ice cream comes in all kinds of shapes, sizes, tastes, and textures . . .
Which one would you like to try?

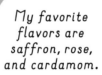

My favorite flavors are saffron, rose, and cardamom.

Italy is the home of **GELATO** *(jell-ahh-toe)*. It's made from milk and cream that are stirred slowly while they're being frozen. This means that it has less air in it than some types of ice cream. The stirring also makes it glossy, dense, and rich. And very, VERY popular.

Classic flavors are often based on the fruits and nuts available — like pistachio in fall, blood orange in winter and spring, and wild strawberry in summer. Oh, and chocolate and caramel all year round!

KULFI *(kul-fee)* is made by cooking milk for a VERY long time — SO long that it becomes sweet! Flavors are added before the milk is poured into a mold and frozen.

It's often eaten on a stick, along with toppings like ground spices or nuts. The smooth, solid, frozen treat is eaten in many countries, including India, Nepal, and Bangladesh.

In some places, the ice cream comes to you! In the UK and the US, small trucks drive around the streets playing music to entice people to buy their frozen treats. A particularly popular ice cream is **SOFTSERVE** — it's silky and squeezed out of a machine directly into a cone. Toppings include chocolate candy, flavored syrup, and sprinkles.

What's YOUR favorite flavor of ice cream?

SHAVED ICE is enjoyed around the world, but especially in East Asian countries such as China, Malaysia, and Singapore. It's sometimes described as "sugary snow" because it can be light and fluffy—and it's served with sweet syrups, condensed milk, jellies, sweetened red beans, and corn.

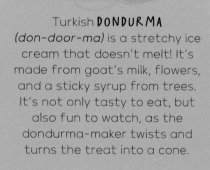

Turkish **DONDURMA** (don-door-ma) is a stretchy ice cream that doesn't melt! It's made from goat's milk, flowers, and a sticky syrup from trees. It's not only tasty to eat, but also fun to watch, as the dondurma-maker twists and turns the treat into a cone.

Who says ice cream has to be sweet? In Japan, people also enjoy savory flavors like *matcha* (green tea), fiery *wasabi*, and purple sweet potato. One way Japanese children eat their ice cream is wrapped in a thin rice cake called **MOCHI** (moh-chee). It's chewy and DELICIOUS!

FANTASTIC FRUIT
What's your favorite fruit?

There are more than 2,000 different types of fruit that you can eat! Humans only really enjoy around 200 of them, and most people only have access to fruit that is grown locally or travels well. All fruits are amazing in their own way, but some that grow in the warmest parts of the world are particularly fabulous to look at and eat. Which would you like to try?

AÇAÍ *(ah-sigh-yee)* **BERRIES** grow in huge clusters at the top of very tall palm trees in the Amazon Rainforest, Brazil.

MAKRUT *(ma-guut)* **LIME** has a sour and bitter juice, and its zest and leaves are often used in Thai dishes.

RAMBUTAN *(ram-boo-tan)* comes from a Malay word that means "hair" — which makes sense when you look at this fruit. But, once you peel the skin, the flesh inside is smooth and sweet.

PITAYA *(pih-tie-yah)* comes from Mexico, Guatemala, and Costa Rica. It's is also known as "dragon fruit" because of its leathery, spiky, and scaly pink skin.

The Chinese fruit **LOQUAT** *(low-kwut)*, also known as *nespolo* and "Japanese medlar," is sweet, tangy, and juicy.

FEIJOA *(fay-zhow-uh)* from New Zealand is an egg-sized fruit that tastes like a sour mix of strawberries, pineapple, and quince.

PASSION FRUIT, is grown in places like Brazil, Colombia and Paraguay, and can be small and purple, or large and yellow. The seeds and pulp inside look like frog eggs, but are incredibly tasty.

When cooked, BREADFRUIT from Papua New Guinea feels like fresh bread and tastes like potato!

MANGOSTEEN *(man-go-steen)* is from Borneo, and is sometimes called the "Queen of fruit." That's because in the 1800s, the British monarch Queen Victoria is rumored to have said she would make anyone who brought this delicious fruit to her a knight.

CACTUS FRUIT from Mexico are also known as "prickly pears." They taste a bit like bubblegum, but you need to peel them . . . OUCH!

TAMARILLO *(tam-a-ril-low)*, also known as a "tree tomato," is an egg-shaped fruit from Colombia. It has a similar texture to tomatoes, but is much more sour.

When it's ripe and orange, PAPAYA *(pa-pie-ya)* from Laos is eaten as a fruit. But, when it's raw and green, it's also used in savory salads.

The most eaten fruits

After tomatoes, the most eaten fruits in the world each year, are:

1 BANANAS
(160 MILLION TONS)

WATERMELONS
(113 MILLION TONS)

APPLES
(94 MILLION TONS)

GRAPES
(88 MILLION TONS)

ORANGES
(82 MILLION TONS)

MANGOES
(44 MILLION TONS)

PLANTAINS
(44 MILLION TONS)

GOING BANANAS!

Take your pick

We eat more bananas than any other fruit! Over 100 billion every year, and about half of those are eaten for breakfast.

The vast majority of bananas eaten by humans are called CAVENDISH BANANAS. They ripen slowly, which means they can be transported around the world before being eaten. They're also difficult to bruise when they're still green. Cavendish bananas weren't always the most popular — we used to prefer the GROS MICHEL (grow-mee-shell), but disease wiped them out. That's one of the problems with relying on just one type of food.

These small, fragrant bananas are grown in Australia and Southeast Asia. They're called PISANG MAS (pee-sang mas) — also known as "lady finger" bananas!

Most bananas are yellow, but not all of them . . . RED BANANAS from Colombia and Ecuador have a maroon skin and a pinky-yellow flesh.

Before they're ready to eat, blue JAVA BANANAS are . . . well, blue! Or at least a silvery-greeny blue. In Hawaii, where they grow, they're sometimes called "ice-cream bananas" because when they're ripe, they have a similar taste and texture to vanilla ice cream. Scrumptious!

PLANTAINS are generally eaten as a savory food and need to be cooked first. In places like Ghana, Cameroon, Haiti, and Indonesia, they are baked, mashed, roasted, or fried like potato chips and fries. It's a REALLY important ingredient and is one of the most popular fruits in the world.

AN APPLE A DAY
From apple strudel to tarte tatin

Apples are popular all over the world: from harvest apple-bobbing in the US to giving apples as a symbol of peace in China. There are thousands and thousands of different types, and lots of traditional apple dishes too.

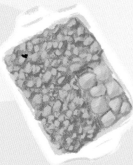
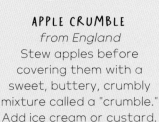

TARTE TATIN (tart ta-tan)
from France
To make a tarte tatin, cook apples in caramel, top them with pastry dough, and bake. Then flip the pan upside down when it's ready to serve.

APFELKÜCHLE
(ap-fel-kookh-luh)
from Germany
Cut slices of apple, dip them in a batter, and deep-fry to make fritters. Make sure you let them cool down a little before taking a bite!

APPLE CRUMBLE
from England
Stew apples before covering them with a sweet, buttery, crumbly mixture called a "crumble." Add ice cream or custard.

APPLE STRUDEL (stroo-del)
from Austria
Pile cooked apples onto pastry dough, roll into a tube, brush with butter, and bake. Add custard or whipped cream.

MILOPITAKIA (mee-lo-pi-ta-kee-a)
from Greece
Place chopped apples onto paper-thin pastry dough and fold into a triangle. Bake until they're golden and crunchy.

BÁNH TÁO HOA HỒNG
(bank tau woa hong)
from Vietnam
Arrange slices of apple onto a pastry so that they overlap, then your little tarts will look just like roses!

TANGHULU (taung-hoo-loo)
from China
Thread crab apples onto a stick, then coat with a shiny, sugary glaze. Yum!

ÆBLEKAGE (ae-bluh-kayge)
from Denmark
Grab a big bowl (or lots of small ones) and build layers of cooked apples, whipped cream, custard, and sponge cake to make an apple trifle. Enjoy!

PASTRIES AND DESSERTS

Which sweet treat would you like to eat?

From flat to puffy, crisp to crunchy, smooth to sticky, here are a selection of pastries and desserts from around the world.

MARITOZZO
(ma-ree-totz-oh)
A ball of sweet, airy dough that's filled with a cloud of cream. It's very popular in Italy.

CHURROS *(choo-ross)*
These tubes of fried dough from Spain are often sprinkled with sugar and served with a little cup of warm, velvety, liquid chocolate for dipping and sipping. Churros are a real treat at breakfast time!

KUNAFEH
(koo-nah-fay)
These round, shallow desserts from Middle Eastern countries such as Egypt are made of stretchy cheese, syrup, and pastry shredded so finely that it looks like a bird's nest!

STROOPWAFEL
(strope-wah-fel)
A popular sweet snack in the Netherlands, these are made of two thin, golden-brown wafers stuck together with syrup.

PARIS-BREST
(pa-ree-brest)
A French pastry in the shape of a wheel, originally made in honor of a bike race. It's light and crunchy and filled with swirls of sweet, nutty cream.

CARDAMOM BUN
These bronze knots of chewy dough from Sweden are layered with sugar and cardamom.

BAKLAVA
(bak-la-vah)
Baklava is eaten in Turkey, Syria, and other Middle Eastern countries. It's made up of layers and layers of thin, brittle pastry, filled with nuts and honey or syrup.

LAMINGTON
Lamingtons from Australia are cubes of sponge cake covered in chocolate and rolled in dried coconut flakes. If you're lucky, there might also be some strawberry jam in the middle!

I always eat gulab jamun on my birthday!

If I could, I would have tebirkes for breakfast every day!

GULAB JAMUN
(goo-lab ja-mun)
In India, milk is used to make small balls of dough, which are deep-fried and then soaked in sweet syrup.

TEBIRKES
(tay-beer-geess)
These Danish pastries are made from layers of smooth, buttery dough folded around a poppy-seed filling — with more poppy seeds on top!

PASTÉIS DE NATA
(pas-tace de na-ta)
These Portuguese flaky pastry tarts have an oozing custard center.

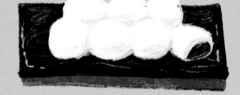

DAIFUKU MOCHI
(die-fu-koo moh-chee)
A small, round, chewy cake from Japan that means "bringer of good luck." It's made by wrapping rice-flour dough around red-bean paste.

PICARONES
(pee-cah-roh-nez)
In Peru, dough rings are made from sweet potato and squash, then deep-fried and drizzled with syrup.

KROŠTULE
(krosh-tule)
In Croatia, people eat deliciously crisp twists and ribbons of deep-fried dough dusted with powdered sugar.

MAKROUDH
(ma-krood)
In Tunisia and other countries in North Africa, little diamond-shaped cookies are filled with date paste. Yum!

MANDAZI
(man-dah-zee)
In Uganda, people enjoy puffy triangles of sweet, fried bread, sometimes served with fruit sauces or a dusting of cinnamon.

MOONCAKE
This Chinese pastry is filled with bean paste. It's traditionally eaten during the Mid-Autumn Festival, also known as the Mooncake Festival.

FUTURE FOODS

What will we eat in the future? What should we be eating now?

For thousands of years, humans have eaten food that has been caught, found, or farmed. But as the population grows (and GROWS) and our climate changes, we can no longer feed the huge number of humans on food that grows "naturally." So what do we do?

Fake food

Farming and fishing on a gigantic scale can't continue forever. That's because in some places the farming is SO intense that it's destroying the land and water it's based on. In other places, extreme weather caused by climate change is making farming more difficult.

Some people think the answer is to grow food in laboratories or factories. These "fake foods" might take less energy, water, and space to make, and would taste and feel similar to meat, fish, vegetables, or fruit.

That means we could soon be eating:

POWDERED FUEL
Powders packed with nutrients include a mixture of fake and natural ingredients and are often flavored by chemicals that taste like fruits and spices. They're more like fuel than food — and when you mix them with water, you get something similar to a milkshake.

LAB-GROWN MEAT
This is meat grown from cells taken from an actual animal. Imagine beef burgers that have a similar taste and texture to normal burgers, but aren't made from a cow! The first lab-grown burger was cooked and eaten in 2013. It took two years to make and cost about $260,000!

"MEAT" MADE FROM PLANTS
These products are made to look and taste like chicken breasts, bacon, beef burgers, and fish fillets, but there's no meat or fish involved. They're made and shaped in factories using ingredients like soybeans and mushrooms.

Incredible insects

Two billion people, mostly living in Asia and Africa, enjoy insects as part of their daily diet. Some people think that everyone should be eating them — it takes much less energy to produce insect meat than, for example, beef or chicken.

At the moment, most humans who dine on insects eat ones that are local, plentiful, and easy to catch. To feed more humans on insects, more countries would need to farm them.

There are actually more than 2,000 edible insects, including worms, flies, and their larva. The most commonly eaten ones are:

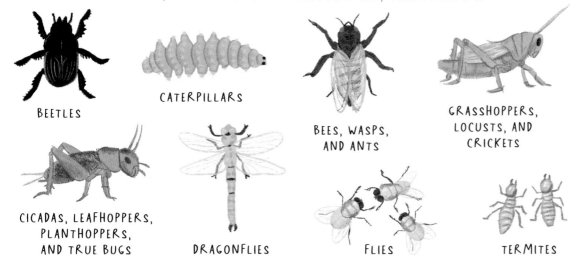

BEETLES

CATERPILLARS

BEES, WASPS, AND ANTS

GRASSHOPPERS, LOCUSTS, AND CRICKETS

CICADAS, LEAFHOPPERS, PLANTHOPPERS, AND TRUE BUGS

DRAGONFLIES

FLIES

TERMITES

Succulent seaweed

In many countries, seaweed is a traditional food. And some scientists think we should eat it more than we do. That's because seaweed is packed with nutrients, and growing it is easy — and may even be good for the environment.

DULSE (dulse)
In Ireland, dulse is used to add a delicious, salty taste to stews, vegetables, and butter.

WAKAME (wa-kaa-mee), **ARAME** (a-ra-may), **AND HIJIKI** (hi-jee-kee) In China and Japan, these seaweeds are shredded and used like vegetables to make tasty, textured salads.

KOMBU (kom-boo) (also known as **KELP**) This is used to flavor many Japanese dishes like miso soup and ramen broths. It's also cut into noodle-like strips and used in salads.

LAVER (lar-ver) (also known as **GIM** and **NORI**) This seaweed is cooked to make a traditional dish in Wales called laverbread. It's also dried and pressed into sheets. In Japan, these are used to wrap sushi, such as *temaki* (or handrolls), and in South Korea, they're deep-fried to make chips called *"gim-bugak."*

BUT before you try gobbling it straight from the ocean . . . Seaweed is VERY salty! So, it's typically soaked or cooked in fresh water before being eaten.

LADHIDH

(la-deed)
In Arabic,
spoken in Algeria

SARR LOTE
GAUNG DAIR

"It is good to eat"
in Burmese, spoken
by some children
in Myanmar

QUÉ RICO

(kay-ree-co)
In Spanish,
spoken in Puerto Rico

HERKULLINEN

(her-kool-li-nen)
In Finnish,
spoken in Finland

DELICIOUS!

Have you enjoyed all this
food?! Here are some
of the ways that children
say "delicious," "yummy,"
or "tasty."

MNOGO
VKUSNO

(mnoh-goh f-kous-noh)
In Bulgarian

O DUNG GAN

(oh dun gon)
"It hits the spot"
in Yoruba,
spoken in Nigeria

MAZEDAR

(ma-zeh-dar)
In Urdu,
spoken in Pakistan

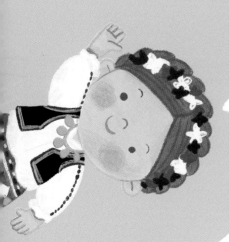

DOVIDENJA
(dov-id-jeh-na)
In Croatian

BAYARTAI
(bi-ya-teh)
In Mongolian

TUPANANCHISKAMA
(too-pan-anchis-kama)
In Quechuan, spoken by some
children in Bolivia

SARA MUSHE
(sara mush-ee)
In Shona,
spoken in Zimbabwe

GOODBYE!
Thank you for sharing
our table. Here are some
words for saying
"goodbye".

ADEUS
(a-dey-osh)
In Portuguese,
spoken in Angola

ÄDDI
(ad-ee)
In Luxembourgish,
spoken in Luxembourg

ADIOS
(a-dee-oss)
In Spanish, spoken
in Nicaragua

MA'A SALAMA
(maa sal-ama)
In Arabic, spoken in
Saudi Arabia

 ALBANIA
 AUSTRALIA
 BALI
 BANGLADESH
 BHUTAN
 BOLIVIA
BOTSWANA
 BRAZIL

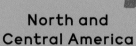

North and
Central America

South America

CAN YOU
POINT TO WHERE
YOU LIVE?

FRANCE
GREECE
ICELAND
ISRAEL
LATVIA
MALAWI
MEXICO
MOROCCO

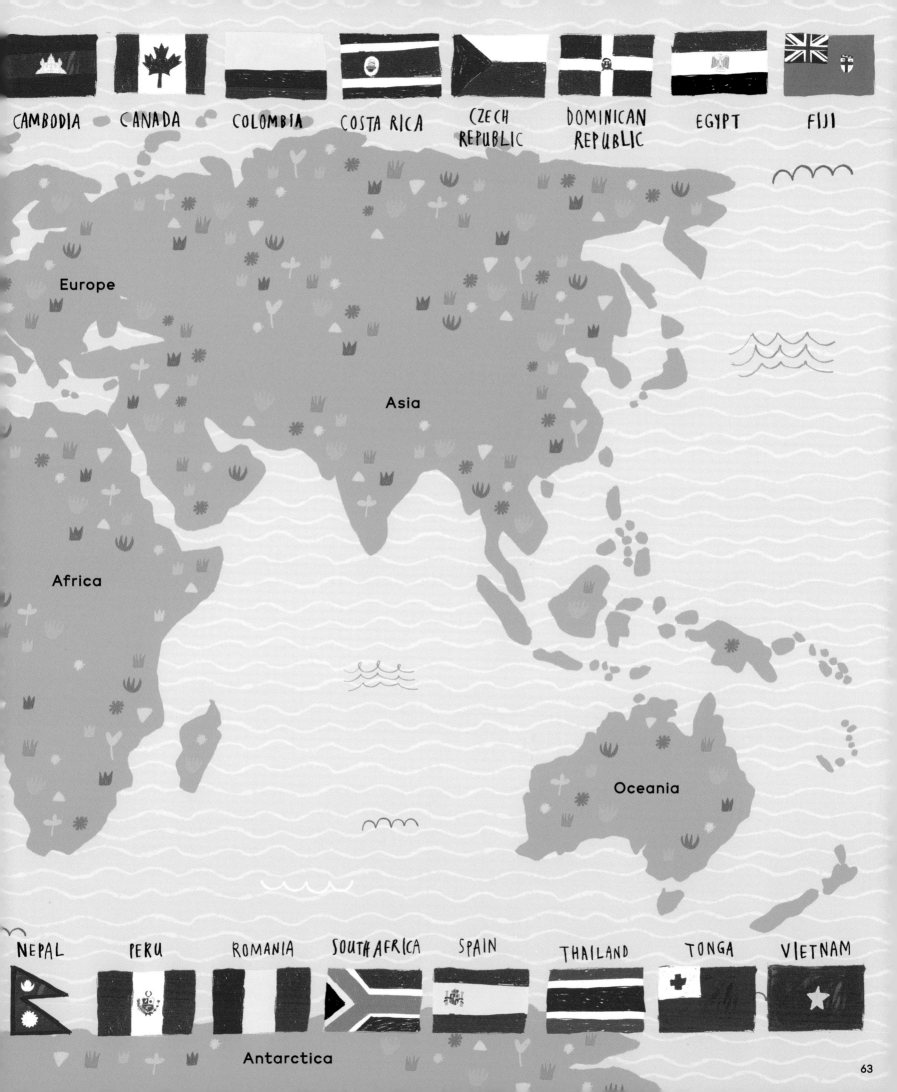

CAMBODIA CANADA COLOMBIA COSTA RICA CZECH REPUBLIC DOMINICAN REPUBLIC EGYPT FIJI

Europe

Asia

Africa

Oceania

NEPAL PERU ROMANIA SOUTH AFRICA SPAIN THAILAND TONGA VIETNAM

Antarctica

63

List of countries and places featured

Afghanistan	Ecuador	Kazakhstan	Saudi Arabia
Albania	Egypt	Kenya	Serbia
Algeria	England	Laos	Singapore
Angola	Eritrea	Lebanon	Slovakia
Antigua	Ethiopia	Libya	Somalia
Argentina	Finland	Luxembourg	South Africa
Armenia	France	Malaysia	South Korea
Australia	Georgia	Maldives	Spain
Austria	Germany	Mexico	Sri Lanka
Bangladesh	Ghana	Mongolia	Sweden
Belgium	Greece	Morocco	Switzerland
Benin	Guatemala	Myanmar	Syria
Bhutan	Haiti	Nepal	Thailand
Bolivia	Hawaii	Netherlands	Trinidad and Tobago
Borneo	Hungary	New Zealand	Tunisia
Brazil	Iceland	Nicaragua	Turkey
Bulgaria	India	Nigeria	Uganda
Cambodia	Indonesia	Norway	Ukraine
Canada	Iran	Pakistan	USA
Cameroon	Iraq	Palestine	Uzbekistan
China	Ireland	Papua New Guinea	Venezuela
Colombia	Israel	Peru	Vietnam
Croatia	Italy	Philippines	Wales
Cyprus	Ivory Coast	Poland	Zambia
Czech Republic	Jamaica	Portugal	Zimbabwe
Denmark	Japan	Romania	

The end

ENDA
(en-da)
Icelandic

SAMĀPTA
(sam-ap-ta)
Nepali

AN DEIREADH
(an der-un)
Irish

OXIRI
(ox-iri)
Uzbek

Y DIWEDD
(er due-eth)
Welsh

FUND
(foo-nd)
Albanian

KONIEC
(kon-yets)
Slovak

SLUTTEN
(shloo-ten)
Norwegian

TE MUTUNGA
(tay moo-toon-ga)
Maori

ANTA
(an-ta)
Gujarati

ENDE
(en-da)
German

SLUTET
(slow-tet)
Swedish

KRAJ
(cry)
Serbian

TAMAT
(tam-at)
Malay

VÉGE
(ve-gair)
Hungarian

FIN
(fan)
French

FIN
(fin)
Spanish

DI SOF
(dee sof)
Yiddish

TMIEM
(tee-min)
Maltese

64